SPOTLIGHT

D0982283

NAVAJO & HOPI COUNTRY

JULIAN SMITH

Contents

NAVAJO AND HOPI COUNTRY 7

Planning Your Time 10

Flagstaff and Vicinity 11
History 11
Sights 13
  (Museum of Northern Arizona 13
  Pioneer Museum 14
  Lowell Observatory 14
  Riordan Mansion State Historic Park .. 15
  The Arboretum at Flagstaff 16
Entertainment and Events 16
  Nightlife 16
  The Arts 16
  Events 17
Shopping 17
Recreation 17
  Hiking 17
  Mountain Biking 18
  Rafting and Kayaking 18
  Skiing 18
  Other Activities 18
Accommodations 19
Food 20
Information 21
Transportation 21
Around Flagstaff 22
  Walnut Canyon National Monument .. 22
  Grand Falls of the Little Colorado 22
  Sunset Crater National Monument 22
  Other Crater Hiking 23
  Wupatki National Monument 23
  San Francisco Mountains 24
  Cameron Trading Post and Gallery ... 25

Sedona 26
History 26
Sights 27
  Chapel of the Holy Cross 27
  (Oak Creek Canyon 27
Events 27
Shopping and Services 27
Recreation 27
  Hiking 27
  Biking 28
  Other Activities 28
Accommodations 28
Food 29
Information 29

Grand Canyon National Park 29
The South Rim 31
  Grand Canyon Village 31
  Accommodations and Food 31
  Getting There 31
(The North Rim 31
  Sights and Hikes 32
  Accommodations and Food 32
  The Kaibab Plateau 32
  Tuweep 32
The Inner Canyon 33
  Hiking 33
  Rafting the Canyon 34
  Tours and Activities 34

Navajo Reservation 35
Tuba City and Vicinity 35
  Sights 35
  Shopping and Events 36
  Accommodations and Food 36

Kayenta and Vicinity 37
  Shopping and Events 37
  Accommodations and Food 37
Navajo National Monument 37
  Sights and Hikes 37
  Accommodations and Food 38
(Monument Valley 38
  Visiting Monument Valley 38
  Goulding's Lodge and Trading Post . . .39
  Oljato 40
(Canyon de Chelly National
  Monument 41
  History 41
  Visiting Canyon de Chelly 43
  North Rim Drive 44
  South Rim Drive 45
  Tours 46
  Chinle 47
  Many Farms 47
Hubbell Trading Post National
  Historic Site 47

Hopi Reservation 48
East of First Mesa 50
First Mesa 51
Second Mesa 51
  Villages 51
  Hopi Cultural Center and Vicinity 51
Third Mesa 52
  West of Third Mesa 53

East of Flagstaff 53

Meteor Crater .53
Winslow 54
  Sights 54
  Shopping 55
  Accommodations and Food 55
  Transportation .55
Holbrook 55
  Sights 56
  Entertainment and Events 56
  Shopping 56
  Accommodations and Food 56
  Transportation .57
Petrified Forest National Park 57
  Visiting the Park 58

Gallup and Vicinity 58
  History 58
  Gallup Today 59
  Sights 59
  Events 60
  Shopping 60
  Recreation 61
  Accommodations 61
  Food 62
  Information and Transportation 62
Window Rock, Arizona 62
  Sights 62
  Shopping 63
  Accommodations and Food 63
  Information 63
North of Gallup 63
  Highway 491 63
  Shiprock 63

NAVAJO & HOPI COUNTRY

NAVAJO & HOPI COUNTRY

The high tablelands of northeastern Arizona, northwestern New Mexico, and southernmost Utah encompass two of the country's largest Native American reservations, as well as one of the Four Corner's most vibrant cities (Flagstaff) near one of the country's most incredible natural sights (the Grand Canyon). These are some of the loneliest yet most extraordinary acres of the Colorado Plateau, averaging between 5,000 and 7,000 feet in elevation. The wide-open country is a textbook of geology: buttes, washes, mesas, volcanic plugs, and dikes break the otherwise flat expanse, but all pale next to the biggest gorge of them all, northwest of Flagstaff. Sagebrush, yucca, and desert grasses march to the rim of deep canyons, and the heights of Navajo Mountain, Black Mesa, and the Chuska Mountains on the Arizona–New

Mexico border are dusted with snow in winter. The largest ponderosa pine forest in the world spreads to both rims of the Grand Canyon, and virtually every hill in sight in the 1,800-square-mile San Francisco Volcanic Field is or was a volcano, some of which have erupted within the past 1,000 years.

But it is the indigenous cultures that truly define this part of the Four Corners. Anasazi cliff dwellings are scattered throughout the region, with those at Navajo National Monument rivaling anything in Colorado or Utah. The Navajo and Hopi tribes have maintained their traditions into the 21st century in the face of almost overwhelming odds. Farming, ranching, herding, and tourism provide an income for many, while mining and logging enrich a few. With the exception of Flagstaff, the

© JULIAN SMITH

© JULIAN SMITH

the Grand Canyon

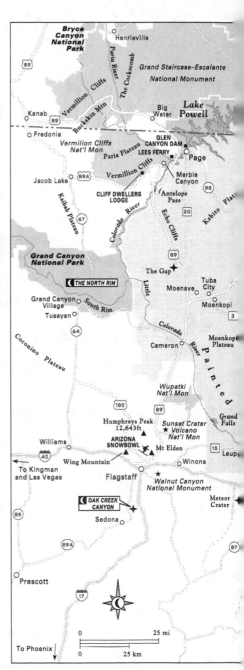

larger cities on or near the reservations, including Tuba City, Kayenta, Window Rock, and Gallup, are not very big, and the surrounding poverty can make them as much sobering as inviting. But there is still much to do: shopping at the many native galleries in Flagstaff and Gallup; taking in breath-stopping views of Canyon de Chelly National Park, Monument Valley, or the Grand Canyon; walking the creaking floors of the Hubbell Trading Post in Ganado; and watching dances in the timeless villages of the Hopi Reservation. Flagstaff alone can keep visitors occupied for weeks, with three national monuments, some of the Southwest's best museums, a ski resort, and trails galore amid the 600-plus volcanic peaks that dot the skyline.

Outside Gallup and Flagstaff, tourist services are few and far between. Most of the towns on the reservations have hotels, but food choices are limited, and it may be an hour or more to the next gas station. Although the reservations are legally dry, alcoholism and drunk driving

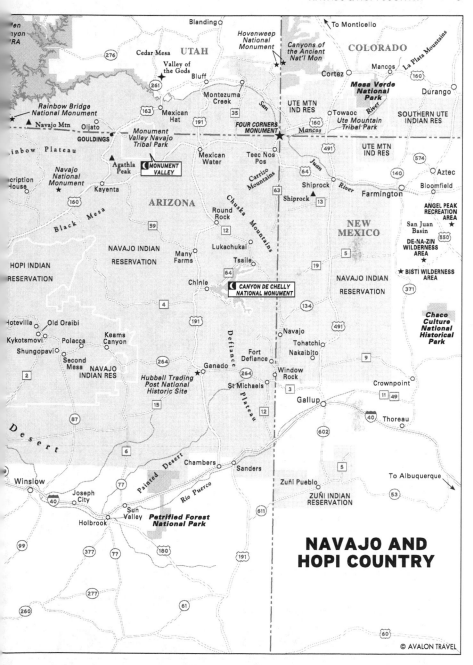

NAVAJO AND HOPI COUNTRY

© AVALON TRAVEL

HIGHLIGHTS

◖ **Museum of Northern Arizona:** An extensive collection, clearly presented, makes this Flagstaff museum a must-see (page 13).

◖ **Oak Creek Canyon:** When you're ready for a break from psychic readings or mountain biking in the red-rock sanctuary of Sedona, this water-filled canyon between Flagstaff and Sedona is a great place to beat the summer heat (page 27).

◖ **The North Rim:** Less visited and cooler in the summer, the Grand Canyon's northern rim seems a world apart from its southern one (page 31).

◖ **Monument Valley:** Towering mesas and buttes make up one of America's best known vistas (page 38).

◖ **Canyon de Chelly National Monument:** A gorgeous canyon system preserves a timeless slice of Navajo life (page 41).

LOOK FOR ◖ TO FIND RECOMMENDED SIGHTS, ACTIVITIES, DINING, AND LODGING.

---

are still serious problems. Keep in mind, too, that you need permission to hike or camp inside an reservation, either from local landowners or the tribal government.

PLANNING YOUR TIME

Flagstaff is the most obvious staging point for an exploration of northern Arizona's Native American country. This piney college town is an appealing place to spend 2–3 days, including at least part of one perusing the collection of the outstanding **Museum of Northern Arizona.** You'll want to take at least a day to visit **Grand Canyon National Park,** although for anything more than the view from the edge you'll need gear, permits, and some strong legs. **Sedona,** down lovely Oak Creek Canyon, is worth another day or two if you plan on

soaking up more than just a bit of the groovy local energy.

The Navajo Reservation has impressive gorges of its own, led by the **Canyon de Chelly National Monument,** whose sandy bottoms are still inhabited after centuries. **Monument Valley** is a visual cliché for good reason: The stone monoliths rising from the flat desert is one of the most amazing sights in the American West.

The railroad towns of Flagstaff, Winslow, and Holbrook are along I-40, which parallels the southern border of the Navajo Reservation. The interstate passes the gaudy palettes of the Painted Desert and Petrified Forest National Park as well, as it continues east to New Mexico and west to California, and I-17 heads south from Flagstaff to Phoenix. Highway

Monument Valley

89 runs north from Flagstaff, splitting off Highway 89A before reaching Page and the Utah border.

Highway 491 (formerly, and infamously, named Highway 666) cuts across the northern border of the Navajo Reservation from Tuba City to Shiprock via Kayenta—actually Highway 64 from Tec Nos Pos. Highway 89 runs north from Flagstaff to Page along the western edge. Crossing the reservation, you have two main choices: Highway 191 up the center, through Ganado and Chinle to Mexican Water, Utah (paralleled by Highway 12 north of Window Rock), and the east–west Highway 264/3, from Tuba City across the Hopi mesas to Ganado, Window Rock, and Gallup. Countless dirt roads reach much of the rest of the reservations, but a large portion remains inaccessible. These tracks can be very rough, particularly in bad weather, and they are seldom marked; the AAA *Guide to Indian Country* map is your best weapon against getting lost.

Flagstaff and Vicinity

"Flag" (pop. 65,000) is and has always been a railroad town—an average of 135 trains still roar through every 24 hours, sounding their whistles by law and dividing the city frustratingly in two for up to half an hour. It's also a city very aware of its heritage, from the historical markers on downtown buildings to the great old neon motel signs on Route 66 out of town. With 20,000 students in residence at Northern Arizona University (NAU), the music, art, and outdoors scenes are all thriving. The pointed San Francisco Peaks tower directly over the city, covered with snow a good part of the year. It may be hard to believe as the heat waves shimmer up off the flat desert below, but at 7,000 feet, Flagstaff is actually the second-snowiest metropolitan area in the country after Syracuse, New York, with an average of 108 inches of snow yearly.

In terms of tourist attractions, there is very little that Flagstaff lacks: skiing the Arizona Snowbowl, hiking the Grand Canyon, visiting the outstanding Museum of Northern Arizona and Lowell Observatory, or taking a day trip to Sedona or a nearby Native American reservation. Three national monuments are within half an hour of the city, making a great loop day trip in themselves.

HISTORY

The Sinagua, less-advanced cultural cousins of the Anasazi, were living in pit houses and canyon-edge dwellings in the foothills of the San Francisco Mountains when major eruptions in 1064 and 1065 covered 800 square miles of the surrounding countryside with lava and ash. They returned soon after to build Anasazi-style pueblos and farm the newly enriched soil, but moved on around the same time the Anasazi did, perhaps for similar reasons.

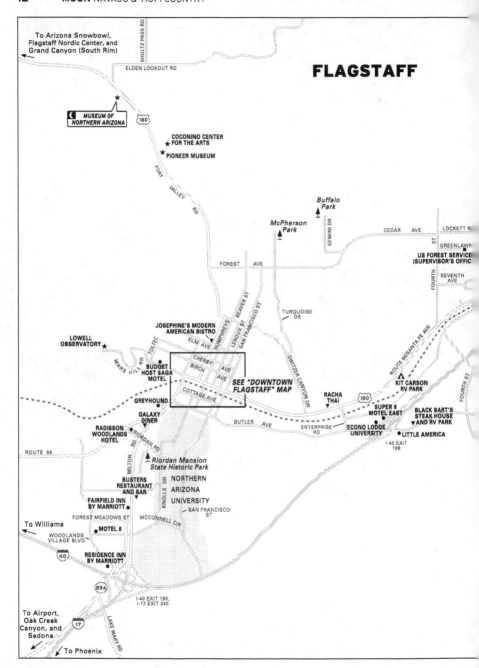

FLAGSTAFF

To Arizona Snowbowl,
Flagstaff Nordic Center, and
Grand Canyon (South Rim)

SHULTZ PASS RD

ELDEN LOOKOUT RD

MUSEUM OF
NORTHERN ARIZONA

180

COCONINO CENTER
FOR THE ARTS

PIONEER MUSEUM

FORT VALLEY RD

Buffalo
Park

McPherson
Park

GEMINI DR

CEDAR AVE

LOCKETT R

GREENLAWN

US FOREST SERVICE
(SUPERVISOR'S OFFIC

FOREST AVE

SEVENTH
AVE

FOURTH

JOSEPHINE'S MODERN
AMERICAN BISTRO

TURQUOISE
DR

LOWELL
OBSERVATORY

ELM AVE

HUMPHREYS

LEROUX ST

BEAVER ST

SAN FRANCISCO ST

MARS HILL RD

ROUTE 66

CHERRY AVE

BIRCH AVE

SWITZER CANYON DR

ROUTE 66/SANTA FE AVE

BUDGET
HOST SAGA
MOTEL

SEE "DOWNTOWN
FLAGSTAFF" MAP

KIT CARSON
RV PARK

GREYHOUND

COTTAGE AVE

RACHA
THAI

180

FOURTH ST

GALAXY
DINER

BUTLER AVE

SUPER 8
MOTEL EAST

BLACK BART'S
STEAK HOUSE
AND RV PARK

RADISSON
WOODLANDS
HOTEL

MILTON RD

RIORDAN RD

ENTERPRISE
RD

ECONO LODGE
UNIVERSITY

LITTLE AMERICA

ROUTE 66

Riordan Mansion
State Historic Park

I-40 EXIT
198

BUSTERS
RESTAURANT
AND BAR

NORTHERN
ARIZONA
UNIVERSITY

KNOLLS DR

FAIRFIELD INN
BY MARRIOTT

SAN FRANCISCO
ST

FOREST MEADOWS ST

MCCONNELL CIR

To Williams

MOTEL 6

WOODLANDS
VILLAGE BLVD

40

RESIDENCE INN
BY MARRIOTT

89A

I-40 EXIT 195,
I-17 EXIT 340

To Airport,
Oak Creek
Canyon, and
Sedona

17

LAKE MARY RD

To Phoenix

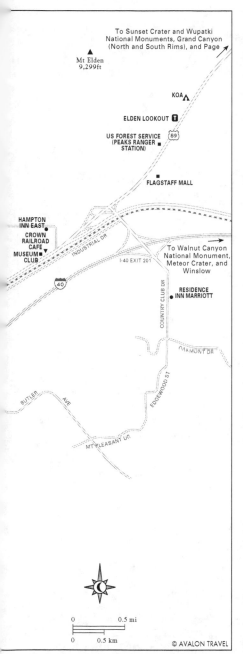

To Sunset Crater and Wupatki
National Monuments, Grand Canyon
(North and South Rims), and Page

Mt Elden
9,299ft

KOA

ELDEN LOOKOUT

US FOREST SERVICE
(PEAKS RANGER
STATION)   89

FLAGSTAFF MALL

HAMPTON
INN EAST

CROWN
RAILROAD
CAFE
MUSEUM
CLUB   INDUSTRIAL DR

I-40 EXIT 201

To Walnut Canyon
National Monument,
Meteor Crater, and
Winslow

COUNTRY CLUB DR

RESIDENCE
INN MARRIOTT

MAMOTH DR

EDGEWOOD ST

BUTLER   AVE

MT PLEASANT DR

0   0.5 mi

0   0.5 km

© AVALON TRAVEL

The area was explored by four separate military surveys before Flagstaff itself came into being. In 1876, a group of settlers arrived from Boston, and on July 4 they raised an American flag on a peeled pine tree in what is now Antelope Park. The early settlement didn't last, but the flagpole did, and travelers heading west were told to keep an eye out for the good campsite it marked. Some of these settlers eventually stayed, and the name stuck. The first post office and the railroad both arrived in 1881, and by 1886 Flagstaff was the biggest city on the railroad line between Albuquerque and the Pacific Ocean. The Arizona Lumber and Timber Company made a fortune from the abundant forests, shipping logs out cheaply by rail. Sheep and cattle ranches provided more jobs.

Coconino County, established in 1891, was soon the second largest in the country. Three years later the Lowell Observatory was built, and in 1930 Dr. Percival Lowell discovered was, until a new designation in 2006, the planet Pluto in Flagstaff's crystal skies. Route 66 and its attendant traffic arrived in the 1920s, allowing more and more visitors to discover the wonders of the Grand Canyon and the Native American reservations nearby.

SIGHTS
◖ Museum of Northern Arizona

Founded in 1928, this outstanding museum (3101 N. Fort Valley Rd., 928/774-5213, www.musnaz.org, 9 A.M.–5 P.M. daily, $7 adults, $4 children) has evolved into the best of its kind in the Four Corners. Displays on anthropology, biology, geology, and fine art are clearly laid out and comprehensive without being exhausting, even though they have more than 600,000 artifacts cataloged. The histories of the Colorado Plateau's tribes are clearly spelled out, and exquisite examples of crafts are on display, including weavings, kachinas, baskets, pottery, and jewelry. Changing exhibits examine topics such as the role of Native Americans in Westerns. The museum's Kiva Gallery contains a mock-up of a Hopi kiva with a beautiful mural by Michael Kabotie

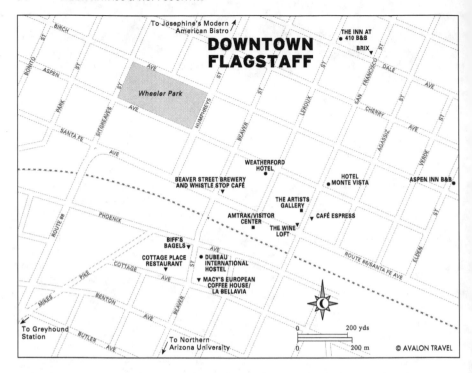

and Delbridge Honanie, covering everything from Buddha and Hopi spirits to the Internet and modern problems of drugs and diabetes. A local nonprofit offers free birds of prey demonstrations daily at noon and 2 P.M. from April through October in the outdoor amphitheater. Special collection tours ($10 pp) are offered on the third Friday of every month. Ideally you'd start your visit to the Colorado Plateau here, on North Fort Valley Road (Highway 180) three miles northwest of downtown Flagstaff.

Pioneer Museum

The 1908 Coconino County Hospital for the Indigent was converted to a boardinghouse and then a museum in 1963. Today, the northern division of the Arizona Historical Society administers the building as a museum (928/774-6272, 9 A.M.–5 P.M. Mon.–Sat., free) on North Fort Valley Road on the way to the Museum of Northern Arizona. The collection includes more than 10,000 bits of Flagstaff's past, from an old iron lung to farm gear and clothing. Nearby are a 1910 barn, a 1912 steam locomotive, and a historic cabin that was moved here from the east side of the San Francisco Mountains. In the blacksmith shop behind the museum, the sweaty craft is demonstrated Thursday–Saturday in summer.

Lowell Observatory

Boston aristocrat-turned-astronomer Percival Lowell founded this observatory (1400 W. Mars Hill Rd., 928/774-3358, www.lowell.edu, 9 A.M.–5 P.M. daily, from noon Nov.–Mar., $5 adults, $2 children) in 1894. He spent 15 years gazing at Mars through the 24-inch refractor telescope, convinced that he was looking at the remains of canals built by an intelligent race. On that matter he was way off, but his hunch about "Planet X" orbiting beyond Uranus proved correct: 14 years after his death in 1916,

Pluto was discovered by Clyde Tombaugh, and Lowell is given most of the credit. Today the privately owned observatory sits at 7,260 feet in the clear mountain air above Flagstaff, and is still used for serious research. The Steele Visitor Center offers tours of the original telescope inside historic Clark Dome, built of native ponderosa pine in the days before power tools, as well as the spectrograph used to prove the universe is expanding, and plates with the first images of Pluto. Evening viewing programs are offered from 8 P.M. Monday–Saturday June–August and from 7:30 P.M. Wednesday, Friday, and Saturday September–May, weather permitting.

Riordan Mansion
State Historic Park
Prominent local businessmen Timothy and Michael Riordan were responsible for the success of the Arizona Lumber and Timber Company near the turn of the 20th century. They each married one of the Metz sisters, cousins of the famous traders the Babbitt Brothers, and in 1904 commissioned the architect of the Grand Canyon's El Tovar Hotel to build them a monumental home of logs and volcanic stone. The mansion (409 Riordan Rd., 928/779-4395, www.pr.state .az.us, 8:30 A.M.–5 P.M. daily, from 10:30 A.M. Nov.–Apr., $6 adults, $2.50 children) is actually two separate homes joined by a common area, and has 40 rooms totaling 13,000 square feet. Timothy's side of what the brothers dubbed *Kinlichi* (Red House in Navajo) is open for tours. Original fixtures and hand-carved American Craftsman–style furniture give a taste of life at the high end in early Flagstaff. Reservations are a good idea for the guided tours, offered every hour in the summer.

FLAGSTAFF CLIMATE

Month	Avg. High	Avg. Low	Mean	Avg. Precip.
January	43°F	16°F	30°F	2.18 in.
February	46°F	19°F	32°F	2.56 in.
March	50°F	23°F	37°F	2.62 in.
April	58°F	27°F	43°F	1.29 in.
May	68°F	34°F	51°F	0.80 in.
June	79°F	41°F	60°F	0.43 in.
July	82°F	50°F	66°F	2.40 in.
August	80°F	49°F	64°F	2.89 in.
September	74°F	42°F	58°F	2.12 in.
October	63°F	31°F	47°F	1.93 in.
November	51°F	22°F	37°F	1.86 in.
December	44°F	17°F	30°F	1.83 in.

The Arboretum at Flagstaff

More than 2,500 species of high-elevation plants thrive at the country's highest research botanical garden (4001 S. Woody Mountain Rd., 928/774-1442, www.thearb .org, 9 A.M.–5 P.M. daily Apr.–Dec., $5 adults, $2 children). The arboretum is at 7,150 feet, which gives it only a 75-day growing season, but they still do an amazing job of raising plants from across the Colorado Plateau. Some 2,500 species are cultivated here, half of which are native to the Four Corners. The collection includes the largest herb garden in the Southwest. Wildflowers are particularly impressive during the summer monsoon season, the best time to visit. Several miles of trails wind through the garden's 200 acres, and hour-long guided tours are given daily at 11 A.M. and 1 P.M.

ENTERTAINMENT AND EVENTS

Nightlife

Built in 1931, **The Museum Club** (3404 E. Rte. 66, 928/526-9434, www.museumclub .com) has evolved into one of the best country-music roadhouses in the United States. Enter through the ponderosa pine archway onto the state's largest wooden dance floor. Five more ponderosas support the A-frame roof, and the mahogany bar in the back dates to the 1880s. Live blues, country, rock, and reggae have included national acts like Willie Nelson and John Lee Hooker.

For more live music try **Mia's Lounge** (26 S. San Francisco, 928/774-3315) and **Flagstaff Brewing** (16 E. Rt. 66, 928/773-1442).

The Arts

NAU's **Richard E. Beasley Gallery** (928/523-3549, 11 A.M.–3 P.M. Tues.–Sat) displays rotating exhibits of contemporary art by students and faculty on the second floor of the Fine and Performing Arts building. Eighteenth-century furniture, glassware, silver, and art fill the **Marguerite Hettel Weiss Collection** on the third floor of the Old Main building. These galleries are both under the

© JULIAN SMITH

Flagstaff's Museum Club is an outstanding roadhouse with music, drinks, and dancing.

auspices of the **Old Main Art Gallery and Museum** (928/523-3471, www.nau.edu/ artgallery, noon–5 P.M. Tues.–Sat) on the northern end of campus, whose varied collection is open to the public.

The **Flagstaff Symphony Orchestra** (928/774-5107, www.flagstaffsymphony.org) has been entertaining northern Arizona audiences since 1949. Performances are held in NAU's Ardrey Auditorium September–April, and tickets are available online.

Events

Flagstaff's **Winterfest** in February rolls together more than 100 snow-themed events, including skiing and sled-dog competitions. May brings the beginning of the Museum of Northern Arizona's **Heritage Program,** which highlights the food, music, dance, arts, and traditions of the Colorado Plateau's diverse cultures all summer long. This includes the **Festival of Hispanic Arts and Crafts** in late May, the **Hopi Marketplace** in early July, the **Navajo Marketplace** in early August, the **Zuni Marketplace** in late August, and the **Festival of Pai Arts** (including the Havasupai, Hualapai, Yavapai, and Paiute nations) in late September.

June is full of events, from the **Gem and Mineral Show** and the **Great Fiesta del Barrio and Fajita Cook-off** to the **Pine Country Pro Rodeo and Parade.** The founding of the city and its country are celebrated during the **Fabulous Fourth Festivities,** which serve as a prelude to the **Flagstaff Summer Fest** the first weekend in August, with artists from across the Southwest. The **Coconino Country Fair** and the **Arts and Crafts Festival** both occur over Labor Day weekend, and the **Flagstaff Festival of Science** (www.scifest .org) comes in late September.

SHOPPING

It makes sense that Flagstaff, surrounded by mountains, deserts, canyons, and rivers, has plenty of good sporting-goods stores. Try **Aspen Sports** (15 N. San Francisco, 928/779-1935), **Babbitt's Backcountry**

Outfitters (12 E. Aspen Ave., 928/774-4775), or **Mountain Sports** (24 N. San Francisco St., 928/226-2885). **Peace Surplus** (14 W. Rte. 66, 928/779-4521) stocks climbing, fishing, skiing, and backpacking gear.

The Artists Gallery (17 N. San Francisco St., 928/773-0958) collects the works of more than 40 local contemporary artists under one roof, ranging from blown glass and painting to sculpture and furniture. Herbs, jewelry, kachina dolls, and baskets are on sale at the **Winter Sun Trading Company** (107 N. San Francisco St., 928/774-2884). For more Native American crafts, try **Puchteca Indian Crafts** (20 N. San Francisco St., 928/774-2414).

RECREATION
Hiking

Beyond the 33-mile **Flagstaff Urban Trails System,** which links the city with Fort Tuthill, hikers and bikers have to look no farther than the San Francisco Peaks to find some of the best trails this close to a city in Arizona. Many of these are in the **Mt. Elden/Dry Lake Hills Trail System** and start from the **Mount Elden trailhead,** near the National Forest Service's **Peaks Ranger Station** (5075 N. Hwy. 89, 928/526-0866). Take Route 66 east out of town until it becomes Highway 89, and look across from the Flagstaff Mall. The trails climb up through boulders and huge junipers and piñon pines. The two-mile **Fatman's Loop** overlooks the city and is named as a warning—you have to be at least somewhat fit to tackle this one. A steep, three-mile trail climbs 2,400 feet and leads to the **Elden Lookout Tower** at 9,300 feet, with views as good as you'd expect.

Buffalo Park on the north side of town serves as a trailhead for the **Oldham Trail,** leading 5.5 miles through aspen, spruce, pines, and fir trees to views over Oak Creek Canyon, Sunset Crater, and the Painted Desert. To get there, take San Francisco Street north, take a right on Forest Avenue, which becomes Cedar, and then a left on Gemini; the park is at the end of the road. The Arizona Snowbowl offers access to a number of trails as well. For more information, pick up a copy of Cosmic Ray's *Favorite Hikes Flagstaff & Sedona,* available locally.

Mountain Biking

Cyclists can tackle the 19.6-mile **Mount Elden Loop,** which circles the mountains clockwise by connecting the Schultz Creek, Little Elden, Pipeline, Oldham, and Rocky Ridge trails. This is a great all-day ride, and most of it is moderately difficult single-track. The trailhead is 3.2 miles north of town on Highway 180; turn right onto Schultz Pass Road (Forest Road 557), then park at the intersection with Mount Elden Road (Forest Road 420) and head north on the Schultz Creek Trail. The **Elden Lookout Road** is another good ride, and one of many in the national forests near town—just make sure to stay out of the wilderness area. For more information on roads among the San Francisco Peaks, see *Around Flagstaff* in this chapter.

Absolute Bikes (200 E. Rte. 66, 928/779-5969) rents full-suspension mountain bikes and cruisers. **Single Track Bikes** (575 W. Riordan Rd., 928/773-1862) is another good source of local riding info, gear, and service.

Rafting and Kayaking

As the closest city to the Grand Canyon proper, Flagstaff is often the base of choice for river-runners out to tackle the rapids of the Colorado River and other waterways nearby. **Canyoneers** (928/526-0924 or 800/525-0924, www .canyoneers.com) traces its origins to 1936, when Norman Nevills first guided a trip down the San Juan River. Their Grand Canyon offerings range from weeklong trips on powered boats ($1,575 pp) to 12-day excursions on oar boats ($2,700 pp).

Tim and Pam Whitney have been running the Grand Canyon since 1973, and in 1986 they founded **Rivers and Oceans** (928/526-4575 or 800/473-4576, www.rivers-oceans.com). Their guided trips include the Grand Canyon and rivers in southern Utah and Idaho. **Arizona Raft Adventures**

(800/786-7238, www.azraft.com) also offers Grand Canyon raft trips. **Canyon Rio Rafting** (800/272-3353, www.canyonrio .com) offers family raft trips on rivers in central Arizona, the San Juan, and the Chama River in northern New Mexico. These range from two hours to all day ($100 adults, $80 children), and they also have gear rentals and kayak instruction.

Skiing

For information on downhill skiing at the Arizona Snowbowl in the San Francisco Mountains, see the *Around Flagstaff* section of this chapter. The **Flagstaff Nordic Center** (928/220-0550, www.flagstaffnordiccenter .com, 9 A.M.–4 P.M. daily Dec.–Mar.) offers over 20 miles of groomed trails ($10 pp) in the national forest, as well as gear rentals ($15–20 pp), refreshments, and instruction ($35 pp including rentals and ski pass). It's 16 miles north of town on Highway 180. Other popular cross-country skiing trails are on Wing Mountain, northwest of Flagstaff via Highway 180 and Forest Road 222B, and Hart Prairie, 9.5 miles northwest via Highway 180 and Forest Road 151.

Other Activities

Four Season Outfitters & Guides (107 W. Phoenix Ave., 877/272-5032, www.fsoutfitters .com) organize hiking, backpacking, climbing, and rafting tours throughout the Four Corners. Day hikes into the Grand Canyon are $145, including transport, food, and park admission, and can be lengthened up to a week and more. Three days in the Escalante canyons are $675 per person. They have a rental/retail shop on the premises, and rent gear, too.

Maxis and Frank Davies have been guiding horseback trail rides into the San Francisco Peaks from their **Flying Heart Ranch** (928/526-2788) for 50 years. They're located next to the Horsemen Lodge about 20 minutes north of downtown on Highway 89, and their rides last from 90 minutes to all day.

ACCOMMODATIONS

As northern Arizona's main tourist center, it's no surprise that Flagstaff has an abundance of lodging options. Rates fall by as much as half in the off-season, and many inexpensive chain motels (some with great old neon signs) line the Route 66 strip on its way out of town.

Under $50

The popular **Dubeau International Hostel** (19 W. Phoenix, 928/774-6731 or 800/398-7112, www.dubeauhostel.com) has dorm rooms for $18–20 and private rooms for $41–48. Breakfast is included, and it's a good idea to book private rooms a few weeks or even a month in advance, especially in the summer. They organize trips to Sedona ($50 pp, Thurs. and Sun.) and the Grand Canyon ($70 pp, Mon., Wed., Fri., and Sat), and offer Internet access, a cable TV/VCR room, and laundry services.

On Route 66, the **Budget Host Saga Motel** (820 W. Rte. 66, 928/779-3631) has rooms for under $50 as well.

$50-100

On January 1, 1900, John W. Weatherford opened a hotel in the dusty frontier town of Flagstaff that still bears his name. The **◖ Weatherford Hotel** (23 N. Leroux St., 928/779-1919, www.weatherfordhotel.com, $85–130) has gone through various incarnations since then—billiard hall, theater, and radio station, to name a few—but after two decades of work it has been restored to its pioneer peak, when Zane Grey wrote *The Call of the Canyon* while staying here. Period touches include a 19-foot lobby ceiling, the wraparound third-floor balcony, and a huge wooden bar in the ballroom, built for a Tombstone saloon over a century ago. (They have rooms with shared bath for $50–70). **Charly's Pub & Grill** offers sandwiches ($8–9), Southwest specialties ($9–11), and dinner entrées for $16–22, as well as live music on weekends.

The **◖ Hotel Monte Vista** (100 N. San Francisco St., 928/779-6971 or 800/545-3068, www.hotelmontevista.com, $65–110) is Flagstaff's other historical (and, purportedly, haunted) lodge downtown. It has hosted presidents and Hollywood stars since it was built in 1927, including John Wayne, who reported a friendly ghost in his room. Most of the 50 rooms on four floors have good views, and all are named after famous guests. There is a day spa on-site, and the cool **Monte Vista Lounge** downstairs has live bands on weekends and the original 1927 bar.

A number of chain hotels fall into this price category, including the **Motel 6** (2475 S. Woodlands Village Blvd., 928/779-3757) and the **Super 8 Motel East** (3725 Kasper Ave., 928/526-0818).

$100-150

Again, it's mostly chain hotels in this range: try the **Econo Lodge University** (2480 E. Lucky Ln., 928/774-7701) or the **Fairfield Inn by Marriott** (2005 S. Milton Rd., 928/773-1300). The **Radisson Woodlands Hotel** (1175 W. Rte. 66, 928/773-8888, $80–150) offers a heated outdoor pool, the Sakura Japanese restaurant, and a café.

Over $150

C. B. Wilson, cousin to Wyatt Earp, built the graceful 1912 home three blocks from downtown that has been turned into the **Aspen Inn Bed & Breakfast** (218 N. Elden St., 928/773-0295 or 888/999-4110, www .flagstaffbedbreakfast.com, $120–160). The owners speak German, Spanish, and Italian (and English).

Some of the nine rooms at **◖ The Inn at 410 Bed & Breakfast** (410 N. Leroux St., www.inn410.com, $170–300) have fireplaces and/or whirlpool tubs. The owners of the 1894 Craftsman home, which was at one time the home of NAU's Sigma Nu fraternity, offer gourmet breakfasts and can arrange two-night packages, including a tour of the Grand Canyon. They've repeatedly won awards as one of the best bed-and-breakfasts in the state.

Situated on 500 acres of ponderosa

pines, **Little America** (2515 E. Butler Ave., 928/779-7900 or 800/865-1401, www.little america.com/flagstaff, $100–200) is a big spread with 247 units decorated with imported marble, a heated outdoor pool and restaurant. For nice suites on the edge of town, head to the **Residence Inn by Marriott** (3440 N. Country Club Dr., 928/526-5555 $150–160). They have one- and two-bedroom suites, all with kitchens.

Campgrounds

All of the following are open year-round. **Black Bart's RV Park** (2760 E. Butler Ave., 928/774-1912) has 174 wooded sites for $20–22 near I-40 exit 198. They also have a saloon, an antiques store, and host a musical revue in the steak house. The **Flagstaff KOA** (5803 N. Hwy. 89, 928/526-9926 or 800/562-3524) offers both campsites ($25–35) and cabins ($45), five miles northeast of town near I-40 exit 201.

You can camp just about anywhere in the national forest that surrounds Flagstaff; just make sure you're not on private land (signs, fences, and houses are good clues), and be very careful with fires in this tinderbox woodland. In the Coconino National Forest, the **Bonito Campground** is on the loop road near Sunset Crater Volcano National Monument, with 43 sites open April–October for $16. Turn left (west) at the Sunset Crater turnoff from Highway 89 onto Forest Road 552 and follow the signs to the **Lockett Meadow Campground,** which has 17 sites at 8,600 feet for $10, open May–October. Call 928/526-0866 for information on both of these.

FOOD

Flagstaff has an amazing variety of places to eat, with plenty of inexpensive options priced for student budgets.

Downtown

Many restaurants are south of the train tracks on Beaver Street, close to NAU. **La Bellavia** (18 S. Beaver St., 928/774-8301, breakfast and lunch daily) is a comfy spot that has earned Flagstaff's "best breakfast" title many times since they opened in 1976. Try their signature Swedish oat pancakes. The smell of fresh-roasted coffee permeates **Macy's European Coffee House, Bakery and Vegetarian Restaurant** (14 S. Beaver St., 928/774-2243, all meals daily) thanks to the big red roaster by the tables. Their creative menu includes many vegetarian and vegan selections, with soups, salads, and sandwiches for $5–6.

A few blocks away **Biff's Bagels** (1 S. Beaver St., 928/226-0424, 7 A.M.–3 P.M. Mon.–Sat., 8 A.M.–2 P.M. Sun.) serves breakfast, coffees, and bagels, with sandwiches in the $4–5 range. They also have Internet access. Stop by the **Beaver Street Brewery and Whistle Stop Café** (11 S. Beaver St., 928/779-0079, lunch and dinner daily) for catfish platters and wood-fired pizzas ($8 and up), or enjoy one of their home-brewed ales on the outdoor patio. There's a billiard room for after dinner, too.

Occupying a restored 1909 bungalow, the (**Cottage Place Restaurant** (126 W. Cottage Ave., 928/774-8431, dinner Wed.–Sun.) may just be Flagstaff's best restaurant. This intimate spot, built in 1909, serves appetizers such as escargots for $8–14 and a wonderful two-person chateaubriand for $77 (à la carte entrées are $24 and up). Their wine list has earned *Wine Spectator* magazine's Award of Excellence six times. Reservations are recommended.

Homemade vegetarian plates are a specialty of **Cafe Espress** (16 N. San Francisco St., 928/774-0541, breakfast and lunch daily, dinner Wed.–Sat.) along with coffees and fresh-baked treats. It's also a gallery that exhibits local artists' works.

One of the newest additions to Flagstaff's dining lineup is **Brix** (413 N. San Francisco St., 928/213-1021, lunch and dinner Mon.–Sat.), a "casual fine dining" restaurant and wine bar in a turn-of-the-century brick carriage house. Their contemporary American menu emphasizes seasonal and farm-fresh ingredients. Entrées like crispy duck's breast and house-made pappardelle pasta are $9–13 for lunch and $23–30 for dinner. There's a well-chosen wine list and wide variety of cheeses to enjoy at the long candlelit bar.

For more wine try **The Wine Loft** (17 N. San Francisco St., 928/773-9463), a wine bar with a light menu served Monday–Friday 3–8 P.M. They offer 40 wines by the glass and Belgian beers, too. At **Josephine's Modern American Bistro** (503 N. Humphreys St., 928/779-3400, lunch Mon.–Sat., dinner daily), gourmet lunch sandwiches are around $10, and dinner entrées run $20–28. Their culinary influences range from southwestern to Asian, but everything is tasty, from the beef tenderloin medallions mole to the soy glazed salmon salad.

Route 66

Sixty-six omelets fill the menu at the **Crown Railroad Cafe** (3300 E. Rte. 66, 928/522-9237, 6 A.M.–9 P.M. daily) next to Museum Club. Lunch and breakfast specials are $4–5, and they have northern Arizona's largest electric train running around the restaurant. (It's one of two in town.) Meat loaf sandwiches, malts, movie posters, and waitresses in Hawaiian shirts sum up the **Galaxy Diner** (931 W. Rte. 66, 928/774-2466, all meals daily), a neon-and-silver faux–Route 66 diner (it's not that old) that does American road staples for $5 and up. The burgers are good, and they serve breakfast all day. An excellent Asian option is **Racha Thai** (1580 E. Rte. 66, 928/774-8390, lunch and dinner Tues.–Sat., dinner Sun.), with candlelit tables and many vegetarian choices. Dinner entrées run $8–15, but they offer lunch specials for $6–7.

Elsewhere in Town

Busters Restaurant and Bar (1800 S. Milton Rd., 928/774-5155, lunch and dinner daily) is an animated place with steaks, seafood, and chicken dishes for lunch ($5–10) and dinner ($10–18). Northern Arizona's finest sushi bar is probably **Sakura**, in the Radisson Woodland Hotel (928/773-9118, lunch Mon.–Sat., dinner daily). They also

serve teppanyaki, with entrées starting at $6 for lunch and $10 for dinner.

If you like music with your prime rib, head to **Black Bart's Steak House and Musical Revue** (2760 E. Butler Ave., 928/779-3142, dinner daily), a Western-themed place abutting an RV park where students in NAU's voice program serenade diners over oak-broiled steaks and chicken.

INFORMATION

The **Flagstaff Convention and Visitors Bureau** (928/774-9541 or 800/842-7293, www.flagstaffarizona.com) runs a **visitors center** in the old train station at 1 East Route 66 (8 A.M.–5 P.M. daily). Find information on the surrounding mountain country, including maps and brochures, at the **Coconino National Forest supervisor's office** (1824 S. Thompson St., 928/527-3600, www.fs.fed.us/r3/coconino, 7:30 A.M.–4:30 P.M. Mon.–Fri) behind the shopping center. They also operate the **Peaks Ranger Station** (5075 N. Hwy. 89, 928/526-0866), open similar hours.

TRANSPORTATION

Flagstaff's local **Mountain Line** bus service (928/779-6624) runs three routes through the city Monday–Friday, and two on Saturday. **Greyhound** (399 S. Malpais Ln., 928/774-4573) takes advantage of the city's location on I-40 with service to major cities to the east and west. **Amtrak** (1 E. Rte. 66, 928/774-8679) has runs to Los Angeles and Albuquerque daily. **Open Road Tours & Transportation** (800/766-7117, www.openroadtours.com) offers daily bus shuttle service to Phoenix ($42 one-way, $76 round-trip) and the South Rim of the Grand Canyon ($27 pp, plus $6 park fee), stopping in Williams. **Flagstaff Express Shuttle Services** (928/225-2290 or 800/563-1980, www.flagstaffexpress.com) also connects Flagstaff with Phoenix (3–4 per day, $34 each way) and the Grand Canyon (2 per day, $24 each way, plus $6 park fee).

From Pulliam Field, five miles south of

town, **US Airways** (www.usairways.com) flies daily to Phoenix. (It's usually cheaper to fly to Phoenix and take a bus from there, or vice versa.) **Horizon Air** (www.alaskaair.com) heads to Los Angeles, Seattle, and Portland.

AROUND FLAGSTAFF
Walnut Canyon
National Monument

This steep, lush canyon south of Flagstaff was home to at least 100 members of the Sinagua ("without water") culture in the 12th and 13th centuries, who built homes in shallow alcoves on the steep walls. The sandstone gorge itself is a wonder, with abundant vegetation and wildlife. Residents raised corn, beans, and squash in fields among the pine forests on the canyon rim, above limestone ledges in the upper canyon dotted with marine fossils. Eventually they moved on; today, some Hopi clans trace their ancestry to Walnut Canyon.

Six miles of the 20-mile canyon are protected today, including more than 300 masonry ruins. The **visitors center** (928/526-3367, www.nps.gov/waca, 8 A.M.–5 P.M. daily May–Oct., 9 A.M.–5 P.M. Nov.–Apr., otherwise 8 A.M.–5 P.M., $5 adults) sits on the edge of the 400-foot-deep ravine, and holds exhibits on the Sinagua culture, a bookstore, and information on ranger-guided hikes given in summer (backcountry hiking on your own is not allowed). The self-guided, mile-long **Island Trail** climbs down into the canyon past the ruins of 25 cliff dwellings. The trail's steepness and the altitude (6,700 feet) make it harder than you'd think. Another short trail leads along the rim past viewing points, a pit house, and a small pueblo.

Keep your eyes peeled for the canyon's varied wildlife, which inhabit several overlapping ecological communities. About 70 species of mammals in the area include coyotes, mule deer, elk, mountain lions, black bears, pronghorn antelopes, and a host of smaller critters. Canyon wrens, Cooper's hawks, prairie falcons, and great gray owls are some of the 121 resident bird species.

To get there, take exit 204 off I-40 and drive south three miles to the visitors center.

A **local passport** to Walnut Canyon, Sunset Crater, and Wupatki costs $25, and is good for one vehicle for a year.

Grand Falls of the Little Colorado

A tongue of lava from Merriam Crater created this 185-foot cascade about 100,000 years ago. It's only worth coming in the spring (or after summer thunderstorms), when meltwater roars over the edge. The falls, which are higher than Niagara Falls, are just over the border of the Navajo Reservation, about 30 miles northeast of Flagstaff. To get there, take exit 245 off I-40 east of Flagstaff, and take Route 99 north to Leupp. From there take Route 15 west to a sign reading Grand Falls Bible Church, where you'll turn right onto a rough road that ends at the river. A 0.25-mile trail heads to the overlook. The dirt roads can be muddy and impassable in bad weather.

Sunset Crater National Monument

Somewhere between A.D. 1040 and 1100, the youngest of more than 600 volcanoes in the San Francisco Volcanic Field started to blow its top. Flowing lava and forest fires lighted the night sky, and residents fled as firebombs rained down and earthquakes shook the ground. When the eruptions subsided people had already begun moving back into the newly fertile area north of the new black peak.

The dramatic cinder cone volcano is 1,000 feet high and nearly a mile wide at its base. Surrounded by deep cinders and lava flows, it is not the most hospitable-looking landscape, but trees, shrubs, and flowers have begun slowly recolonizing the scorched habitat. The name comes from the multicolored mineral deposits on the crater rim that seem to light up at sunset.

A 36-mile **loop road** off Highway 89 north of Flagstaff connects Sunset Crater (8,029 feet), the Strawberry Crater Wilderness (in the Coconino National Forest), and Wupatki National Monument. It's a lovely drive through a landscape of black- and rust-colored volcanic debris, sagebrush, and juniper. Sunset Crater Volcano is on the southern end of the loop; turn right 12 miles north of Flagstaff and go two more miles to the newly renovated **visitors center** (928/526-0502, www.nps.gov/sucr, 8 A.M.–5 P.M. daily May–Oct., 9 A.M.–5 P.M. Nov.–Apr., $5 adults), where you can find a bookstore, picnic tables, and information on daily guided walks and evening programs. The entrance fee is good for a week both here and at Wupatki. Across the road is the U.S. Forest Service's (USFS) **Bonito Campground** (928/526-0866, mid-May–mid-Oct., $16). One of the monument's two trails begins a mile east of the visitors center. The steep **Lenox Crater Trail** goes 0.5 mile to the top of a cinder cone, and will have the less fit gasping for air by the end. Another 0.5 mile down the loop road is the beginning of the **Lava Flow Trail,** a mile-long loop past sharp lava flows, spatter cones, lava tubes, and cinder drifts like black snow. There is also a 0.25-mile paved wheelchair-accessible trail through this landscape.

A **local passport** to Walnut Canyon, Sunset Crater, and Wupatki costs $25, and is good for one vehicle for a year.

Other Crater Hiking

Just east of the Sunset Crater visitors center is the road leading to the O'Leary Group Campground and the seven-mile round-trip trail to the fire tower on top of **O'Leary Peak** (8,965 feet). This lava-dome volcano offers excellent views of the Painted Desert and the San Francisco Volcanic Field, including Sunset Crater.

Farther north up the loop road is the 10,141-acre **Strawberry Crater Wilderness,** centered on yet another cinder cone and its accompanying lava flow. It's much older the Sunset Crater, formed between 50,000 and 100,000 years ago, and the wilderness area is full of prehistoric ruins. Indigenous residents used volcanic cinders as a sort of mulch to hold water, to make up for the area's dry location in the rain shadow of the San Francisco Peaks. (Only about seven inches of precipitation fall here every year)

The easiest access to the area is from Highway 89. About 16 miles north of the Flagstaff Mall, take Forest Roads 546 and 779 east to the wilderness boundary, where an unmarked trail leads to the summit. You can also enter the wilderness area from the loop road to the east.

Wupatki National Monument

The only place in the Southwest where at least three separate cultures overlapped, Wupatki preserves four multistory pueblos, including the largest in the Flagstaff area. They rose during the 12th century A.D., when residents returning after the eruption of Sunset Crater Volcano found the soil much improved by the water-retaining ash and cinders. The Wupatki Basin bears the distinct signs of the Sinauga, Cohonina, and Kayenta Anasazi cultures, who arrived during a period of general population rise throughout the Southwest. By the mid-13th century, however, they had moved on to the north, east, and south, where they were assimilated into the cultures of those areas.

The Wupatki **visitors center** (928/679-2365, www.nps.gov/wupa, 9 A.M.–5 P.M. daily, $5 adults) is 14 miles from the northern end of the loop drive. There's a picnic area, vending machines, and a bookstore available, and exhibits inside on the various cultures that met and coexisted more or less peacefully here. A reconstructed pueblo room gives you an idea of life in the distant past. Entrance is good for a week both here and at Sunset Crater. Ask about orientation programs and guided hikes, given occasionally in summer and more often in spring and fall.

A short self-guided trail leads to the multistory **Wupatki Pueblo** on a side branch of Deadman Wash. This 100-room structure is built from red stone that contrasts with the black lava and green vegetation. The trail circles the pueblo, passing rooms on the far side that were once used to house rangers.

The Wupatki Pueblo near Flagstaff had over 100 rooms.

Nearby are a reconstructed Mexican-style ball court—the northernmost one yet found—and a blowhole, a small opening to an underground chamber that expels or draws in air depending on barometric pressure.

A side branch from the loop road leads 2.5 miles to **Wukoki Pueblo,** which may have housed two or three families and is the monument's best-preserved pueblo. Farther north on the loop road are three smaller pueblos. The 30-room **Citadel Pueblo** stands like a castle on a small butte, near **Nalakihu Pueblo,** about half as big. **Lomaki Pueblo** sits on the edge of a small box canyon, and had nine rooms between two stories.

A **local passport** to Walnut Canyon, Sunset Crater, and Wupatki costs $25, and is good for one vehicle for a year.

San Francisco Mountains

The most distinctive features of Flagstaff's skyline were named by Franciscan monks after St. Francis of Assisi, the founder of their order, as they went about their holy business on the Hopi Reservation. The Navajo consider it Doko'oosliid ("abalone shell mountain"), the Sacred Mountain of the West. The Hopi term is Nubat-i-kyan-bi ("place of the snow peaks"), and believe their kachina spirits live among the summits for part of every year, before flying to the Hopi mesas in the form of nourishing rain clouds. The play of light over the amazingly symmetrical peaks makes it easy to see why the Hopis revere them—the 1930s Works Progress Administration (WPA) guide to Arizona wrote, "At sunrise they appeal gold; at noon they are Carrara marble against a turquoise sky; at sunset they are polished copper, ruby, coral, and finally amethyst."

The range tops out at **Humphrey's Peak,** Arizona's highest point at 12,633 feet, and is home to a ski resort and miles upon miles of trails. Many of these are inside the 18,960-acre **Kachina Peaks Wilderness,** which encloses most of the highest peaks north of Mt. Elden. A huge caldera formed during the mountain's most recent eruption (about two million years ago) forms an inner basin filled with aspens, pines, and firs. As you can imagine, the views from up here are fabulous, from flower-covered meadows all the way down to the Painted Desert and, if it's a clear day, the Grand Canyon.

The easiest way to get into the heart of the hills is the road to the **Arizona Snowbowl** (928/779-1951, www.arizonasnowbowl.com), which leaves Highway 180 seven miles north of downtown and climbs another seven uphill. In the winter, 32 mostly intermediate runs are served by four lifts and a towrope. All-day lift tickets are $48–52 adults, $26–30 children 8–12; instruction and rentals are also available.

In summer, the chairlift (10 A.M.–4 P.M. daily Memorial Day–Labor Day, weekends Labor Day–mid-Oct., $12 adults, $8 youth, under seven free) still runs to the 11,500-foot peak. It operates from late June to Labor Day, and Friday–Sunday until mid-October. The Agassiz Lodge Restaurant offers a deli-style menu for lunch and live music on Saturday afternoons. Two excellent trails leave from the lower parking lot; the five-mile **Kachina Trail** is a good, moderate hike south to Schultz Pass, and the six-mile **Humphrey's Peak Trail** leads above the tree line to Humphrey's Peak. (Note that hiking is not allowed off trails above 11,400 feet to protect the fragile tundra vegetation.) The **Schultz Pass Road** is a gravel route connecting Highways 180 and 89 between Mt. Elden and the wilderness area. This 26-mile drive traverses ponderosa forests, open glades, and streams perfect for an afternoon picnic. It's open April–November, weather permitting, and offers access to the **Weatherford Trail,** built by hand in 1926 and popular with families for its gentle grade and views. This trail crosses the Fremont Saddle (11,354 feet) before connecting with the Humphrey's Peak Trail from the Arizona Snowbowl. The western end of the Schultz Pass Road joins Highway 180 just north of the Museum of Northern Arizona. It begins as Forest Road 420, and heads left (north) where the Elden Lookout Road heads right (east).

Another good drive through the mountains is the **Around the Peaks Loop,** a 44-mile gravel route around Humphrey's Peak that's also open April–November, weather permitting. Like the Schultz Pass Road, it is particularly pretty in autumn when the aspens are turning gold. To do the loop counterclockwise, drive 14 miles north of Flagstaff on Highway 89 to Forest Road 418, go west 12 miles to Forest Road 151, and then south 8 miles to Highway 180, 9.5 miles north of Flagstaff.

Cameron Trading Post and Gallery

In 1911, a suspension bridge was built over the Little Colorado River about 50 miles north of Flagstaff. Five years later, Hubert and C. D. Richardson established a trading post where the Navajo and Hopi exchanged wool, blankets, and livestock for dry goods. Today the Cameron Trading Post and Gallery (800/338-7385 or 978/679-2231, www.camerontradingpost.com) is owned by Joe Atkinson, grandnephew of the Richardsons, who has remodeled the old place into a beautiful enclave that's the perfect home base for a Grand Canyon visit.

About a mile north of the intersection of Highways 89 and 64, the Cameron Trading Post has a lodge with 66 rooms ($70–110) featuring hand-carved furniture and balcony views of the Little Colorado Gorge. Many rooms are arranged around the hotel's exquisite gardens, where Chinese elms, fruit trees, and rosebushes were originally planted by Hubert's wife Mabel. A large stone fireplace, pressed-tin ceiling, and native crafts from throughout the Southwest decorate the dining room, serving all meals daily.

There's a food market, gas station, RV park ($15), and post office elsewhere in the complex, and an active trading post where locals buy craft supplies and sundries and sell wool and piñon nuts. Make sure you don't miss the gallery, which has an outstanding collection of antique and contemporary native art. Rugs, concho belts, pottery, kachinas, baskets, and Old West memorabilia fill the place from wooden floor to wide-beamed ceiling. More pieces are on display upstairs, in a series of rooms restored to look like living quarters.

Sedona

South of Flagstaff on Highway 89A is one of Arizona's more famous and unique destinations. Part art center, part resort retreat, and part New Age nexus, Sedona (pop. 10,000) is blessed with unearthly red-rock scenery, a moderate climate at 4,500 feet, and (according to many) a number of spiritual energy "vortexes" scattered among the stones. With more hypnotherapists, masseuses, yoga teachers, spirit guides, life coaches, and artists per capita than any other place in the West, if not the country—not to mention spas and luxury accommodations galore—Sedona makes for a fascinating and wonderfully scenic short trip from Flagstaff.

Getting there is half the fun. Highway 89A follows Oak Creek Canyon most of the 30 miles from Flagstaff to Sedona, an amazing drive past rock monoliths, swimming holes, viewing points, and secluded resort lodges. It gets very crowded on summer weekends, so consider coming at some other time if you can. The same applies to Sedona itself; it's definitely not off the beaten track, with some four million people making the pilgrimage every year.

History

The Hohokam people were the first to live in this arid area, which they improved for cultivation by digging irrigation canals, from roughly 300 B.C. to about A.D. 1450, when they left abruptly and mysteriously. Small groups of Maricopa and Pima Indians arrived later to the banks of the Salt and Gila Rivers.

Sedona's first Anglo settler was J. J. Thompson, who homesteaded across from what is today the Indian Gardens Store in 1876. More settlers followed with cattle and horses, digging irrigation ditches to water crops and raise orchards. The homestead of Frank Pendley is now Slide Rock State Park in Oak Creek Canyon, and his original irrigation system still works. Author Zane Grey helped popularize the landscape with his novel *The Call of the Canyon*, and Smithsonian Institution scientists explored local cliff dwellings near the turn of the 20th century. The remote ranching and farming settlement was finally named after the wife of settler T. C. Schnebly, who chose his spouse's name while establishing the town's first post office out of love and the fact that it was short enough to fit on a cancellation stamp.

Hollywood arrived in the 1940s and 1950s, and in the ensuing decades a new cadre of visitors was drawn by the town's stunning location. Artists, tourists, and retirees came for the scenery and stayed for a variety of reasons, and Sedona gradually became one of the top destinations in the Southwest. The New Age movement of the 1980s brought a new influx of seekers. The city was incorporated in 1988, and half of the 19-square-mile city still belongs to the government in the form of the Coconino National Forest. High-end tourism has begun to replace the desert-love-in vibe of Sedona's early years, but spirituality is still the name of the game.

Cool off during the summer heat at Slide Rock State Park in Oak Creek Canyon.

Sedona is roughly divided into two parts along Highway 89A: "West Sedona," a quieter, residential section, and the more touristy "uptown" to the north, where 89A meets Highway 179.

SIGHTS
Chapel of the Holy Cross
Sedona's famous Chapel of the Holy Cross (780 Chapel Rd., 928/282-4069) seems to be anchored into the red rock itself, 200 feet above the valley, by a huge cross. The Catholic chapel is open to people of all faiths, who come for the spiritual energy that seems to pervade the place and the views, especially at sunset (except in summer when it closes at 5 P.M.). From uptown, take Highway 179 south toward the village of Oak Creek for three miles, then turn left on Chapel Road.

◖ Oak Creek Canyon
Multicolored stone cliffs and pine forests above lush riparian habitat make Oak Creek Canyon one of the most inviting spots in this dry state. Take a dip in Oak Creek at **Slide Rock State Park** (928/282-3034, 8 A.M.–7 P.M. daily in summer, $10 per car, $2 on foot or bicycle), where you can, of course, slide down smooth rocks and hike on three short trials. The park is 10 miles north of Sedona. There are six Forest Service campgrounds in the canyon as well as numerous picnic areas.

EVENTS
In early March is the **Sedona International Film Festival** (www.sedonafilmfestival.com), a multiday event with workshops and independent movies. **Sedona Jazz on the Rocks** (www.sedonajazz.com) brings great music and master classes in September. In early October is the two-day **Sedona Arts Festival,** with over 150 artists and craftspersons.

SHOPPING AND SERVICES
Sedona is chock-full of art galleries and shops selling everything from T-shirts to fine art. A good place to start is the **Tlaquepaque Arts & Crafts Village** (336 Hwy. 179, 928/282-4838,

© ELIZABETH JANG

Tlaquepaque was built to look like a Mexican village.

www.tlaq.com), an imitation Mexican village with more than 40 galleries and shops as well as four restaurants with outdoor dining. Many galleries are concentrated along Highway 179, including **Exposures International Gallery of Fine Art** (561 Hwy. 179, 928/282-1125 or 800/526-7668). Stock up on all things spiritual at the **Sedona Crystal Vortex** (271 N. Hwy. 89A, 928/282-3543), where you can have a psychic reading or a massage.

Sedona's **Center for the New Age** (928/282-2085, www.sedonanewagecenter.com) is on Highway 179 across from the Tlaquepaque shopping plaza, where they offer guided vortex tours, psychic readings, and massage therapy.

RECREATION
Hiking
On a more earthly plane, Sedona is outstanding in the outdoors department. Dozens of hiking trails wind among the red-rock formations. Two great options are accessed off Dry Creek Road (Forest Road 152), which leaves Highway 89A three miles west of the Y. To reach **Devil's**

© JULIAN SMITH

Hiking to one of Sedona's energy "vortexes" is fun whether or not you believe in them.

Bridge, a two-mile out-and-back stroll to one of Sedona's many natural arches, turn right onto the dirt Forest Road 152, two miles from Highway 89A and go 1.3 miles to the marked trailhead. Keep going another 2.5 miles on Dry Creek Road to Boyton Pass Road on your left, which you take another 1.2 miles to the trailhead to **Doe Mountain,** a 3.6-mile out-and-back climb up a mesa with great views.

If it's an energy vortex you're after, head to **Boyton Canyon** by turning right instead of left toward Boyton Pass. The trailhead is near the private Enchantment Resort. The entire canyon is said to be an energy hot spot, but Boynton Spires, reached by the Vista Trail on the right shortly after starting the hike, is a particular spiritual hot spot. In any case, it's all beautiful. **Cathedral Rock** is said to be another vortex, and is a fun slickrock scramble/climb around regardless. (Acrophobes should think twice.) Head south on Highway 179 from the Y intersection for 0.6 mile to the trailhead. For more information on Sedona's great hiking, pick up a copy of Cosmic Ray's *Favorite Hikes Flagstaff & Sedona,* available locally.

Biking

Mountain bikers should head to **Absolute Bikes** (6101 Hwy. 179, Ste. C, 928/284-1242, www.absolutebikes.net/sedona) for rentals ($30–70 per day), sales, and service as well as trail information. **Mountain Bike Heaven** (1695 W. Hwy. 89A, 928/282-1312, www .mountainbikeheaven.com) leads tours on the area's 200 or so miles of trails.

Other Activities

Prefer a motorized adventure? Try **Red Rock Western Jeep Tours** (270 N. Hwy. 89A, 928/282-6826 or 800/848-7728, www .redrockjeep.com), whose four-wheel-drive tours start at $40 per person for 1.5 hours.

ACCOMMODATIONS

In this luxury resort town, you can choose from dozens of outstanding bed-and-breakfasts. The ❰ **Canyon Villa Inn of Sedona** (40 Canyon Circle Dr., 800/453-1166, www.canyonvilla .com, $200–350) is probably the best, with rooms designed around their peerless views of Bell Rock and Courthouse Butte, an outdoor heated pool, and gourmet breakfasts, as well as afternoon hors d'oeuvres. The **Casa Sedona B&B Inn** (55 Hozoni Dr., 800/525-3756, www.casasedona.com, $200–310) is another AAA four-diamond option, with more of a cowboy/Western flavor.

If your budget permits, you can opt for a place like the **Enchantment Resort** (800/826-4180, www.enchantmentresort .com, $300 and above) at the mouth of Boynton Canyon. The setting alone is enough to knock your socks off, with red rock buttresses all around, but the Southwest-leaning cuisine at the Yavapai Restaurant and the services at the Mii Amo spa definitely will.

If it doesn't, there's always the **Village Lodge** (105 Bell Rock Plaza, 928/284-3626, $50–90), or the fun-to-say **Lo Lo Mai Lodge** (50 Willow Way, 928/282-2835, $87–110).

FOOD

Sedona's food choices are as varied as its lodging options, with a local twist; even the McDonald's here forgoes the usual golden arches in favor of a mellower, pastel green "M" on a pink stucco wall. The **Oaxaca Restaurant** (321 N. Hwy. 89A, 928/282-4179, all meals daily) offers the appeal and food of Sonora, Mexico and a rooftop cantina to boot. Mexican entrées are $7–12 for lunch and $10–17 for dinner, and there are more than 50 varieties of tequila at the bar.

The innovative American cuisine of **The Heartline Cafe** (1610 W. Hwy. 89A, 928/282-0785, lunch Fri.–Sun., dinner daily) has earned it repeat best-restaurant honors. The feel is casual but the food is anything but; entrées run $8–12 for lunch and $15 and up for dinner. The **Blue Moon Cafe** (6101 Hwy. 179, Ste. B, 928/284-1831, all meals daily) is a breakfast-all-day kind of place, with hand-tossed pizzas and great Philly cheesesteaks.

An elegant dining spot hidden in an upscale shopping plaza, **Rene at Tlaquepaque** (336 Hwy. 179, Ste. 118, 928/282-9225, lunch and dinner daily) has an extensive wine list and tempting continental selections. Entrées are $8–13 for lunch, $18–28 for dinner. Buffalo and rattlesnake are both on the menu at the southwestern-themed **Cowboy Club** (241 N. Hwy. 89A, 928/282-4200, lunch and dinner daily), a lively spot that occupies one of Sedona's oldest buildings.

The award for Sedona's classiest dining spot goes to **((L'Auberge de Sedona** (301 L'Auberge Ln., 928/282-1661 or 800/272-6777, all meals daily), one of the Southwest's premiere fine dining restaurants, serving elegant French dishes inside or more relaxed bistro fare on the outdoor Terrace on the Creek (April–October). Five-course prix fixe meals are one option ($65–85), or à la carte entrées for $25 and up.

INFORMATION

For more information on Sedona and the surrounding area, contact the **Sedona Chamber of Commerce** (1 Forest Rd., 928/282-7722 or 800/288-7336, www.visitsedona.com).

Grand Canyon National Park

Northwest of Flagstaff stretches one of the world's natural wonders, a mile-deep chasm carved into the high desert by the relentless force of flowing water. Over tens of millions of years, the Colorado River has eaten away the surface of the Colorado Plateau, leaving the canyon to end all canyons: 277 miles long and up to 18 miles wide, with countless side gorges each of which could be a national park in itself. It's one of the country's greatest tourist draws, and justifiably so. The view from the edge is something you'll never forget, and a trip to the bottom—particularly a raft voyage through the famous Colorado River rapids—is almost beyond words.

In addition to the National Park Service, the Grand Canyon Scout website (www.grandcanyon scout.com) is a good source of information.

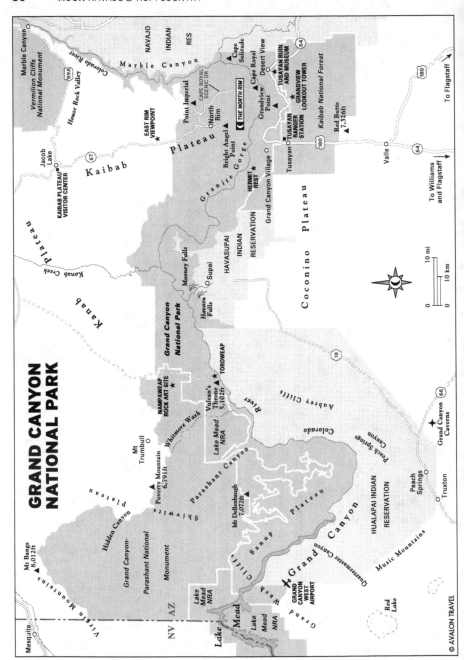

GRAND CANYON NATIONAL PARK

© AVALON TRAVEL

The Colorado River is barely visible at the bottom of the Grand Canyon.

THE SOUTH RIM

Most visitors approach the canyon from this side, which offers the quickest access from major cities (Flagstaff and Phoenix). As a result, the South Rim has more tourist amenities than the more remote North Rim.

Grand Canyon Village

Highway 64 runs north from Williams on I-40 to Grand Canyon Village, the largest settlement in the park. Here you'll find **park headquarters** (928/638-7888, www.nps.gov/grca, $25 per vehicle for one week), a post office, a bank, medical services, numerous stores and gift shops, and the **Canyon View Information Plaza** at Mather Point (8 A.M.–5 P.M. daily).

The Rim Trail offers access to many excellent viewing points over the vastness of the canyon and its tributaries. Highway 64 runs east from Grand Canyon Village for 25 miles along the edge of the canyon, where it's called East Rim Drive inside the park. Along the way are ruins, viewing points, and the **Desert View Watchtower,** a stone structure designed by Mary Colter for the Fred Harvey Company in 1932 and lined with Hopi murals. Highway 64 continues east to Cameron.

Accommodations and Food

Six national park lodges offer accommodations, including the grand old **El Tovar,** built in 1905. Rooms range $166–300, depending on season. For reservations, contact Xanterra Parks & Resorts (303/297-2757 or 888/297-2757, www.grandcanyonlodges.com). Most of the lodges have restaurants. You can camp at the **Mather Campground** (877/444-6777, www.recreation.gov, $18, open year-round) and its attached **Trailer Village** ($25) in Grand Canyon Village, or else the **Desert View Campground** ($12, open May–Oct.), 26 miles east.

More tourist services are available at **Tusayan,** on Highway 64 outside the park boundary.

Getting There

Shuttle services in Flagstaff runs daily buses to Grand Canyon Village and Tusayan. Otherwise, to get to the South Rim you'll have to drive or call a taxi. From Williams, you can take the charming **Grand Canyon Railway** (800/843-8724, www.thetrain.com), which has been chugging along since 1901. The 2.25-hour ride includes roving musicians, a bar car, and a train robbery. Various packages including lodging at the Grand Canyon Railway Hotel Williams are available, but the ride itself is $65–170 per person ($35–100 children).

THE NORTH RIM

Though only about 10 miles from the South Rim as the raven flies, the less-developed North Rim is more than 200 miles away by road, so it sees far fewer visitors. You can still depend on the same stupendous views and the same precipitous trails—you'll just have several thousand fewer people to share them with. Plus, since it's over 1,000 feet higher, it's significantly cooler in summer.

Sights and Hikes

Your first stop, after you've tasted the view, should be the **North Rim Visitors Center** (8 A.M.–6 P.M. daily May–Oct).

A 23-mile **scenic drive** leads to the overlook at **Point Royal**, passing half a dozen more viewing points along the way, many with picnic areas and short trails.

Day hike choices include the 0.5-mile paved **Bright Angel Point Trail,** the 3-mile **Transept Trail** from the lodge to the campground, and the 5-mile **Uncle Jim Trail** to another overlook.

Accommodations and Food

Built in 1928, the log-beam **C Grand Canyon Lodge North Rim** boasts two porches and an octagonal sunroom with huge windows to take advantage of the panorama. Rooms are $115 and cabins start at $120 per night, and it's a good idea to make reservations as far ahead of time as possible through Forever Resorts (877/386-4383,

The geological layers of the Grand Canyon show how it was carved out over eons.

© JULIAN SMITH

www.grandcanyonlodgenorth.com). The same goes for the restaurant, which serves all meals, as well as the **North Rim Campground** (877/444-6777, www.recreation.gov) with sites for $18–25, showers, laundry facilities, a grocery, and a camping store.

The Kaibab Plateau

Highway 89A climbs into the cool evergreen forests of the Kaibab Plateau, and at almost 8,000 feet hits Jacob Lake, where it joins with Highway 67 toward the northern edge of the abyss. The **Jacob Lake Inn** (928/643-7232, www.jacoblake.com) has a restaurant and year-round rooms ($107–136) and cabins ($91–134). It's also where you'll find the **Kaibab Plateau Visitor Center** (928/643-7298, 8 A.M.–5 P.M. daily May–Oct.) run by the Forest Service.

Across the road, **Allen's Outfitters** (801/644-8150 or 928/899-1165) organizes horseback trips into the Kaibab National Forest, and the USFS **Jacob Lake Campground** has primitive sites for $12. A quarter mile south is the **Kaibab Camper Village** (928/643-7804, $15–31) with full hookup sites open May–October. From here, Highway 67 reaches almost 9,000 feet as it winds through the parklike meadows and pine-clad hills of the Kaibab National Forest, one of the prettiest in the lower 48. Buried by snow in winter, the road is open mid-May–mid-October, weather permitting.

Tuweep

For the slightly more adventurous, this "back door" to the North Rim of the Grand Canyon offers something that may seem unbelievable if you've ever been to the South Rim in tour-bus season: solitude. To get there you'll have to negotiate about 60 miles of dirt roads; turn off onto BLM Road 109 (the "Sunshine Route") from Highway 389 about seven miles west of Fredonia, and don't try it with a low-slung car or when it's wet. There aren't any tourist facilities (or water), just a lonely ranger station, but you can drive literally to the edge of the canyon—which looks more like a gorge here rather than a mountain range seen from above—and camp for free, often with only a handful of

© JULIAN SMITH

The remote Tuweep entrance to Grand Canyon National Park lets you have it all to yourself.

other people around. It's a whole other way to experience the Grand Canyon.

The 1.5-mile **Lava Falls Trail** offers the shortest route to the Colorado River from the rim in the entire park. It's steep and rough going over lava, but at the bottom you can watch rafters tackling Lava Falls, the meanest in the park. Eleven primitive campsites (first-come, first-served) are available near the rim, with picnic tables, fire grates, and composting toilets. Contact the North Rim of the park or the park website (www.nps.gov) for more information.

THE INNER CANYON

First, the warnings: Since it gets hotter as you descend into the gorge, and it typically takes twice as much time, energy, and water to climb back out, *and* it can hit over 100°F down there in summer, you should carry at least one gallon of water per person per day from spring to fall. And don't go unprepared, gear- and fitness-wise. It's frighteningly easy to underestimate how challenging hiking in the Grand Canyon

is. The combination of altitude, steep terrain, and lack of water claims victims every year.

The best times to venture into the canyon are in spring and fall; March, April, October, and November are ideal. From May to September, temperatures at the rim can be in the 90s, and in the canyon can climb to over 100°F.

Permits are necessary for overnight camping in the backcountry ($10 plus $5 pp per night). These can be requested in person, by fax, or by mail, but be warned that the park receives about 30,000 requests every year and only grants 13,000. So, file early—up to four months ahead, on the first of the month. See the backcountry hiking portion of the park's website (www.nps.gov) for more details.

Hiking

From the South Rim, the **Bright Angel Trail** heads 9.3 miles downhill to **Phantom Ranch** at the river. Dorm rooms here (segregated by sex) are $36, and meals are also available. An overnight permit is not required at the ranch; reserve rooms through Xanterra (303/297-2757 or 888/297-2757, www.grandcanyonlodges .com). A wealth of other trails lead down into the gorge. One popular hike is the **Grandview Trail** from Grandview Point to Horseshoe Mesa, an old Native American route improved by miners (six miles round-trip).

From the North Rim, you can take the **North Kaibab Trail** 15 miles from Bright Angel Point to Phantom Ranch. The steeper **Bill Hall Trail** also goes all the way to the river, 10 miles and 5,200 feet down. Near the bottom it passes **Thunder River,** which gushes out of a sheer limestone cliff before flowing right into the Colorado, making it by some estimates the shortest in the world.

Rafting the Canyon

Riding the rapids of the Colorado River ranks high up on the list of Things You Should Do Before You Die. Follow in the footsteps of daring explorers as you explore side canyons, float the placid stretches, shrink in significance next to billions of years of geology, and—here the footsteps end—enjoy gourmet meals and the luxury of sleeping bags on a sandbar beneath the stars. Companies in Page, Flagstaff, and other cities in Utah and Arizona offer many different options for running the river, which is a good thing, considering the waiting list for private permits is over a decade long. Choose from motorboats or the classic oar-powered dories, and either the full 226 miles from Lees Ferry to Diamond Creek or a partial trip. The full journey takes 11–19 days by oar or 6–8 days with a motor, or you can join or leave a trip at Phantom Ranch, cutting your travel time considerably.

For more information, see the appropriate listings under *Flagstaff* or see the website of the **Grand Canyon River Outfitters Association** (www.gcroa.org).

Tours and Activities

Besides boot leather, another classic way to enter the canyon is on a **mule ride.** These stout animals have carried visitors up and down the canyon's trails for over a century. These start at $154 per person for a day trip to Plateau Point on the South Rim, and you can go to Phantom Ranch and back for $420 and up per person, including food and accommodations. Contact

gearing up to raft the Colorado River through the Grand Canyon

Xanterra (303/297-2757 or 888/297-2757, www.grandcanyonlodges.com) for reservations and information.

The **Grand Canyon Field Institute** (928/638-2485 or 866/471-4435, www.grand canyon.org/fieldinstitute) organizes a wealth of guided, educational overnight trips into the canyon March–November.

Helicopter tours of the canyon have been a contentious subject, with the machines' noise and intrusiveness jarring visitors who came to get away from it all. If you can't resist, **Maverick Helicopters** (928/282-2980, www .maverickhelicopter.com) operates special quiet-technology helicopters with leather seats and wraparound views. Flights depart from the South Rim and cost $185–245 per person for 25–45 minutes.

Navajo Reservation

TUBA CITY AND VICINITY

One of the Navajo Reservation's most diverse communities, Tuba City (pop. 8,500) sits off Highway 89 between Flagstaff and Page. It was named by early Mormon settlers after a Hopi called Tuuvi, chief of the Water and Corn Clans at Orabi. Tuuvi was the first Hopi to meet Brigham Young, and after converting to the Mormon faith in Salt Lake City, he donated a plot of land to the church on the condition that Mormon settlers would protect the Hopi from Navajo and Paiute raiders. Jacob Hamblin, the "Buckskin Missionary," helped establish a settlement at a well-watered area called Moenave at the foot of a cliff to the north. Mormons heading south along a trail blazed by Hamblin to the Little Colorado River valley often stopped here to rest and resupply. (The trail became known as the Honeymoon Trail, since young Mormon couples had to travel all the way back to St. George, Utah, to have their wedding vows officially solemnized by the church.) The last Latter-Day Saint left Moenave near the turn of the 20th century, when the area was added to the Navajo Reservation.

Although predominantly Navajo, Tuba City has many residents who belong to the Hopi and other tribes, as well as Anglos. The Basha's grocery store serves as the unofficial community gathering place. Although most travelers zip past on their way to the North Rim of the Grand Canyon without a second glance, Tuba City is worth a detour for its shopping and its Navajo tacos.

Sights

Next to the Tuba City Trading Post, the **Explore Navajo Interactive Museum** (Main St. and Moenave Rd., 928/283-5441, 8 A.M.–6 P.M. Mon.–Sat., noon–6 P.M. Sun., $9 adults, $6 children) holds exhibits on the tribe's history and culture, including crafts and the Navajo Code Talkers of WWII.

Tuba City sits on a mesa north of Highway 160 in one of the most striking expanses of the **Painted Desert.** About two miles east on Highway 160 from Highway 89, a dirt turnoff leads to the top of a small hill, a great place to take photos and enjoy the view.

Three more miles brings you to another turnoff marked by a hand-lettered sign for **Moenave,** the site of the original Mormon

THE BETTING WAY

After years of wrangling over whether to take the plunge (and how to split the profits between tribal and local governments), the first Navajo casino opened in 2008 in Church Rock, just east of Gallup along I-40. The 27,000-square foot building houses 350 slot machines, table games, an entertainment venue, and a small café. Alcohol will be served, a first for the reservation. It's planned to be the first of six, two in New Mexico and four in Arizona.

settlement. Near the turnoff are a set of **dinosaur tracks** laid down by the nine-foot Dilophosaurus in the late Triassic mud. Navajo children are usually on hand to give you a short tour (a small tip is expected), and will point out the three-toed footprints, petrified eggs, and even an embedded claw. The settlement of Moenave itself, at the base of Hamblin's Ridge, is a green oasis fed by springs. John D. Lee, of Lees Ferry, hid out here for a while before being tracked down and executed for his role in the Mountain Meadows Massacre.

Shopping and Events

The **Tuba City Trading Post** (928/283-5441, 8 A.M.–6 P.M. Mon.–Fri., 8 A.M.–5 P.M. Sat., 9 A.M.–5 P.M. Sun.) was built in 1870 out of local blue limestone and logs from the San Francisco peaks. Teddy Roosevelt stayed here in 1913 on his way back from hunting mountain lions on the North Rim of the Grand Canyon, and Zane Grey also stopped by. Today, the two-story octagonal showroom holds a wealth of quality crafts, particularly jewelry.

Every Friday the **Tuba City Flea Market** coalesces behind the Community Center. A little bit of everything is for sale—car parts, used clothing, medicinal herbs, turquoise jewelry—and you can listen to the lilting sounds of the Navajo language over a bowl of mutton stew and frybread when you need a breather. The **Western Navajo Fair** is held in the Rodeo and Fair Grounds every October, on the first weekend after Columbus Day.

Accommodations and Food

Next to the Tuba City Trading Post, the **Quality Inn** (928/283-4545) has rooms for $100–125, a restaurant serving all meals, and an RV park with six tent sites. Students at the Greyhills Academy High School run the 32-room **Greyhills Inn** (928/283-6271, ext. 142, $62), as part of a training program in hotel management. Back at the intersection of Highways 160 and 264, the **Tuba City Truck Stop Cafe** (928/283-4975) is a must-eat for road-food gourmands. They boast the "Best Navajo taco in the Southwest," and the messy, heaping concoction of beans, lettuce,

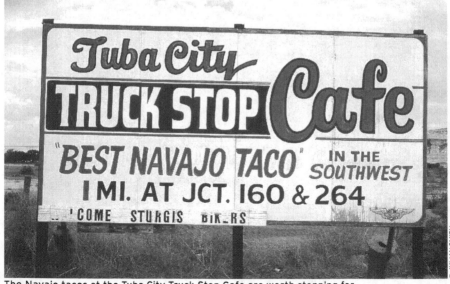

© JULIAN SMITH

The Navajo tacos at the Tuba City Truck Stop Cafe are worth stopping for.

tomatoes, and cheese on top of frybread is hard to beat. Navajo matriarchs decked out in their best jewelry sit beneath signed photos of various celebrities who have stopped in for a bite.

KAYENTA AND VICINITY

The largest city (pop. 5,000) in the northern part of the Navajo Reservation takes its name, loosely, from the Navajo word *teehindeeh,* meaning "bog hole" or "natural game pit," after the gluelike soil around a nearby spring that mired livestock. In truth, it's not the most inviting place, with little of interest besides a few motels, inexpensive restaurants, and a shopping center at the intersection of Highways 160 and 163. It's a dusty town of pickup trucks and cowboy hats, home to miners and farmers. (The Navajo also call it Tódíneeshzheé, meaning "water spreading out like fingers" and referring to nearby springs.)

Shopping and Events

Crafts, Western wear, and craft supplies are sold at the **Navajo Arts and Crafts Enterprises** outlet (928/697-8611, 9 A.M.–6 P.M. Mon.–Fri. in summer, 8 A.M.–4 P.M. Sat., 10 A.M.–4 P.M. Sun.) near the main intersection. The Fourth of July brings the **Todineeshzee Fourth of July Rodeo and Fair** to Kayenta.

Accommodations and Food

Kayenta has only a few chain hotels, all near the main intersection, including the **Best Western Wetherill Inn** (928/697-3231, $80–140) and the **Holiday Inn** (928/697-3221, $90–170).

At the main intersection in town, the **Blue Coffee Pot** (928/697-3396, 6 A.M.–9 P.M. Mon.–Fri.) is a local favorite. Named after a type of container that was once common on the reservation, it serves good steaks, Mexican, and Navajo dishes for $5–9. About 10 miles west on Route 160 is the **Reuben Heflin Restaurant** (928/697-3170, dinner daily), serving seafood, steak, and Southwest dishes in front of the fireplace. You can buy food at the Kayenta Trading Post, a supermarket down the hill behind the Best Western.

NAVAJO NATIONAL MONUMENT

Twenty miles south of Kayenta, Highway 564 leads north to this small monument that protects three of the most impressive and intact Anasazi ruins in the Four Corners. Start at the **visitors center** (928/672-2700, www.nps.gov/nava, 8 A.M.–6 P.M. Memorial Day–Labor Day, otherwise 9 A.M.–5 P.M., free) on the Shonto Plateau nine miles north of Highway 160. It contains a museum, bookstore, and local Navajo artists demonstrating their crafts on occasion.

Sights and Hikes

Two short, easy trails lead to overlooks above the **Betatakin** cliff dwellings, but to really experience the monument you should take a ranger-led tour, offered from spring through fall. This is a little more of an undertaking—the trails are steep and sandy—but both are well worth it.

Betatakin is a five-mile hike, and **Keet Seel** is 17 miles from the visitors center, meaning you can stay the night or do the whole thing in an epic, one-day push. Either way, you can follow a ranger through this 100-room settlement tucked under a cliff overhang. The inhabitants kept their stored food safe from rodents in ingeniously sealed storage chambers. Stone slabs fit perfectly into small doorways, and were held in place by poles slid through wooden loops set into the masonry on either side.

© JULIAN SMITH

The Keet Seel ruin at Navajo National Monument once had over 100 rooms.

Accommodations and Food

The monument has two free **campgrounds,** one with 31 sites and another with 11 sites. The closest lodgings to the monument are in Tsegi Canyon, about 14 miles southeast on Highway 160. Here the **Anasazi Inn Tsegi Canyon** (928/697-3793, www.anasaziinn.com) has 57 rooms ($60) and a small café serving all meals daily. It's nothing special, room-wise, but you can't beat the setting in the pink sandstone gorge.

◖ MONUMENT VALLEY

Driving north of Kayenta on Highway 163 toward the Utah border, and it's easy to feel like you entered a Western movie sunset just as the credits started to roll. Rising from the flat plain like the gods' own rock garden, the stone monoliths of Monument Valley are the unmistakable symbol of the American West, imbedded in the imagination of the world by countless movies, photos, and car commercials.

The Navajo consider all of *Tsébii' nidzisgai* (the "valley within the rocks") to be one huge hogan, with the traditional east-facing door situated near the visitors center. Tribe members sought refuge here during Kit Carson's campaign in the 1860s, and many still live and farm here. Despite the valley's near-mythic status, visitation is limited to a single loop road and permitted tours. (Rock climbing is forbidden, despite what you saw in *The Eiger Sanction* or *Vertical Limit*.) More prosaically, the buttes of Monument Valley are formed of Cedar Mesa Sandstone on top of sloping bases of Halgaito Shale. Over the millennia, the softer shale has eroded more quickly, causing the sandstone to fracture vertically into the towering formations. Many are capped by ledges of red Organ Rock Shale.

Visiting Monument Valley

At an intersection on the state line, a short road leads east to the **Monument Valley Navajo Tribal Park visitors center** (435/727-5870, www.navajonationparks.org, 6 A.M.–8 P.M. daily, 8 A.M.–5 P.M. Oct.–Apr., $5 pp). Here you'll find a snack shop, gift shop, and a

Camping at Monument Valley offers some outstanding views.

restaurant upstairs. There's a desk where you can sign up for a tour, and dozens of local operators have set up booths in the parking lot, offering trail rides, hikes, and vehicle tours through the monument. One of them, **Sacred Monument Tours** (435/727-3218 or 928/380-4527, www .monumentvalley.net), has hiking, jeep, and horseback riding tours starting at $57, with an all-day horseback riding tour for $300 per person. Longer tours leave the loop road for obscure petroglyphs and ruins. **Roland's Navajoland Tours** (928/697-3524) out of Kayenta also does Monument Valley tours. (A large hotel, The View, plans to open November 2008 near the visitors center; see the website http://monument valleyview.com for details.)

The visitors center is perched on the edge of the sandy valley filled with massive square buttes, including the Totem Pole, Castle Rock, the Stage Coach, and the famous Mittens. There are 100 campsites in the **Mitten View Campground**—sites 24 and 25 have the best views, making it well worth getting up for sunrise. Group, tent, and RV sites are available ($10), along with coin-operated showers open in season.

From here the 17-mile **loop road** descends into the valley, past many Navajo homes and a viewing point named for John Ford, who brought this place to the attention of the world in his films. Allow at least two hours for the dirt road, which is good enough for most two-wheel-drive vehicles and closes shortly before sundown. It's also a great mountain bike ride.

For the classic road-trip shot of Monument Valley—the place where Forrest Gump finally stopped running—approach from the north on Highway 191, which changes to Highway 163 in Arizona. A little over 13 miles north of the Utah border there's a small hill, with the highway heading straight as an arrow toward the valley below. Trust me—you'll recognize the view.

Goulding's Lodge and Trading Post
Opposite the valley at the state-line intersection is a complex centered around a trading post opened in the 1920s by Harry Goulding

© JULIAN SMITH

Goulding's Lodge is a slice of Old West (and classic Hollywood) history.

and his wife "Mike" in a 10-person tent. Harry, called **Dibé Nééz** ("tall sheep") by the Navajo, purchased 640 acres at the base of Black Door Mesa in 1937 for $320. Goulding bought local crafts, settled disputes, and acted as a liaison between the Navajo and the government. He also persuaded director John Ford that the local scenery would make an ideal movie backdrop, hoping to bring jobs to the area during the Great Depression. The rest is celluloid history. The valley has been used as the backdrop for countless movies, including the classic Westerns *Stagecoach, My Darling Clementine,* and *Fort Apache.* As Hollywood started to arrive, the Gouldings opened a lodge that became a second home to stars like John Wayne. Movie memorabilia and trading-post artifacts fill the original trading post, which has been turned into a museum (open daily year-round). A suggested donation of $2 is put toward scholarships for local children.

The immaculate, modern **lodge** (435/727-3231, www.gouldings.com) has 62 rooms ($155–190 in season) and the

Stagecoach Dining Room, built for the filming of *She Wore a Yellow Ribbon.* There's a VCR in each room where you can watch the many Westerns available for rent—or just look out from your balcony for the real thing. A modern **campground** has views of the valley as well, along with a heated indoor pool, coin laundry, hot showers, and a grocery store. It's also open year-round, with sites for tents ($24) and RVs ($38). Sign up at the lodge for Navajo-guided **tours** to nearby ruins, petroglyphs, crafts demonstrations, and movie locations.

Oljato

Eight miles past Goulding's is one of the most authentic trading posts left on the reservation, and one of my personal favorites. The **Oljato Trading Post & Museum** (435/727-3390, http://a-aa.com/monumentvalley), was built in 1921, making it one of the oldest in existence. In 2005, they were closed "for now," but the owners still offer trail rides of the area; call first. The drive out here is still worth it for the scenery and the external ambiance alone.

If you find them open, step past the rusting gas pumps into the U-shaped bull pen for everything from hose clamps to ice cream sandwiches. In the back are museum pieces and old photo albums.

◖ CANYON DE CHELLY NATIONAL MONUMENT

Joseph Campbell, international guru of mythology, once called this canyon system in northeast Arizona "the most sacred place on earth." There is definitely something special about this place that makes it stand out even among the Four Corners' scenic and historical marvels. Covering 130 square miles of precipitous gorges and fertile canyon bottoms, Canyon de Chelly (de-SHAY) has the ageless quality of a place inhabited for thousands of years, as Navajo families farm and tend orchards and herds of animals beneath soaring stone monoliths. It's almost as if a pane of glass had been laid across the cliff tops, preserving a way of life that once came dangerously close to extinction. The Navajo still own the land that comprises the monument, which is administered by the National Park Service. Roads run along the canyon's north and south rim, with sweeping overlooks that take in rock spires, Anasazi ruins, and farmland. Aside from one trail to the bottom, the only other way to break the glass floor is to join a Navajo-led tour.

The monument comprises three ravines—Monument Canyon, Canyon del Muerto, and Canyon de Chelly—whose rims range 5,000–7,000 feet in elevation. Down the center runs the Rio de Chelly, from its beginnings in the Chuska Mountains in the east to the mouth of Canyon de Chelly near the town of Chinle, "the place where the water flows out." The glowing red sandstone walls are over 1,000 feet high in places, and as sheer as the side of a skyscraper. Temperatures range from well below 0°F in winter to over 100°F in summer, but the river-deposited sediments and reliable water supply make the canyon bottom excellent for farming. Side streams dry up in summer and rage with flash floods during the summer rainy seasons and spring snowmelt. Quicksand is often a concern in wet, sandy spots.

History

People have lived in this sheltered canyon system for millennia, starting with the Basketmaker-phase Anasazi, who left some 700 ruins here between about A.D. 350 and 1300. They pecked hand and foot trails in the stone faces and progressed from pit houses to apartment-style stone dwellings in alcoves, similar to those at Navajo National Monument, but on a smaller scale. Plentiful rainfall from A.D. 1050 to 1150 let the population grow significantly, with as many as 800 people living in the main canyon. This bounty was short-lived, though—a regional drought during the 1200s lowered the water table and dried up the canyon's streams, forcing the Puebloans to move on.

The Hopi tribe occupied the Canyon de Chelly sporadically thereafter, but by 1700 the Navajo had taken over. They named the place Tséyi', meaning "within the rocks," but it is the Spanish mispronunciation of the word that has stuck. From the Hopi, the Navajo acquired dry-farming techniques (peacefully) and women

Spider Rock towers above the bottom of Canyon de Chelly.

© JULIAN SMITH

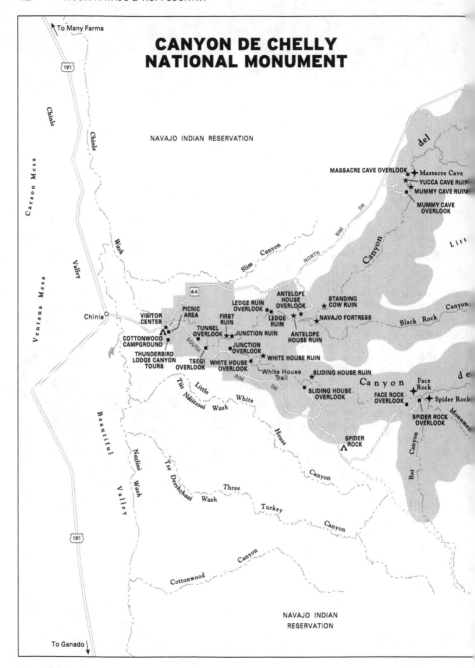

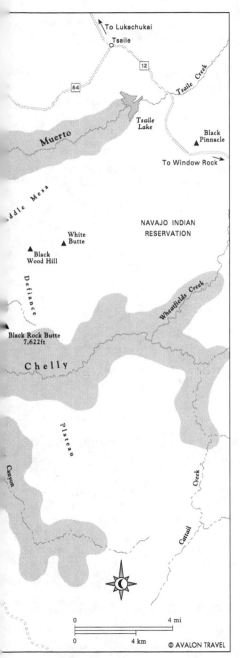

and food (by force), and from the Spanish they stole livestock and horses. Members of many tribes fled here after the Pueblo Revolt of 1680, but it was the Navajo who suffered most during Kit Carson's merciless campaign against them in 1863. Carson's men swept the length of the canyon, laying waste to the orchards and slaughtering livestock. After a brave but futile resistance, the survivors were forced on the Long Walk to eastern New Mexico. The U.S. government signed a peace treaty with the tribe in 1864.

The canyons were declared a national monument in 1931, under a rare arrangement in which management is shared by the tribe and the National Park Service. The Navajo still grow melons, corn, beans, and squash on the fertile canyon bottom, where sheep and goats wander among cottonwoods and peach orchards.

Visiting Canyon de Chelly

Just east of the town of Chinle, a seasonal wash of the same name marks the beginning of the canyon system. You can only descend the rough road leading down into the canyons if you're on a guided tour or if you're a resident. At the **visitors center** (928/674-5500, www.nps.gov/cach, 8 A.M.–5 P.M. daily), three miles west of Chinle, are exhibits on the area's history and geology, as well as restrooms and drinking water. Entrance to the monument is free, as is a spot at the pleasant **Cottonwood Campground,** open year-round. (There is also a privately owned campground on the South Rim Drive.) Nearby is the beautiful **Thunderbird Lodge** (928/674-5841 or 800/679-2473, www.tbird lodge.com), which began as a trading post built by Sam Day in 1902. The original post building is now the cafeteria, decorated with Navajo rugs. Frybread, chili stew, and other tasty bites are available for all meals daily. The lodge is open year-round, with 73 rooms for $106–111 and suites for $152 (lower rates in winter) and a gift shop with a selection that would make Day proud. They also offer tours of the canyon.

Canyon de Chelly consists of four main gorges, and many side canyons, slicing generally eastward into the Defiance Plateau. From a car you can only access the northern and southern edges, but the fantastic views almost make up for the limitations. Short trails lead to the cliff edges. Be careful at the overlooks, there are sharp drop-offs and on occasion car thefts; don't leave anything of value in plain view. The two rim drives would make an excellent bicycle ride, except for the complete lack of anything approaching a bike lane.

North Rim Drive

Also called Highway 64, this road runs along the Canyon del Muerto, connecting Chinle to the Dine College and Tsaile on Highway 12. The canyon was named the Canyon of the Dead in Spanish by a Smithsonian anthropologist who excavated many buried bodies among its ruins. Seven miles in you'll reach the **Antelope House Overlook,** above a ruin named for pictographs of running antelopes painted by a Navajo artist around 1830. The ruins themselves, and artwork left by the Anasazi, are over than a thousand years older. Directly across the canyon, above the junction of the Canyon del Muerto and Black Rock Canyon to the south, is the **Navajo Fortress,** an aerie where Navajo warriors hid from the Spanish and the U.S. military, sneaking down at night for water and food. Just upcanyon

---

NAVAJO CRAFTS

The Diné tell how Spider Woman taught their ancestors to weave on looms built by her husband. The introduction of curly-horned Churro sheep by the Spanish in the 17th century, along with the embracing of pueblo-style looms and a more sedentary lifestyle, allowed the tribe to become expert weavers. Today their **rugs** can hold their own among the world's finest handmade textiles. Women traditionally own the sheep and weave the rugs, which can take months to make. (The Churro sheep was almost extinct by the 1970s, and is being pulled back from the brink through careful breeding.)

Navajo rugs combine Mexican stylistic influences with geometric designs and representations of natural phenomena. At the advice of early Anglo traders, the weavers expanded their repertoire to include brighter colors and more intricate patterns, as well as synthetic yarns. True Navajo rugs, however, are woven from sheep wool, and a quick sniff will reveal an earthy aroma. Other things to look for in a quality rug include symmetry, straight edges, even coloration, and a tight, flat weave. You'll often find a "spirit line" running to the border in older

rugs, included to keep the weaver's spirit from being trapped inside the pattern.

Patterns include the geometric Two Grey Hills, made of natural white, gray, and brown wool; the warm pastels of the Burnt Water style; the elaborately banded Wide Ruins; and the self-explanatory Eye Dazzlers and Pictorials. Sometimes rug patterns are dictated by the color of their background, from Dinnebito (black) to Ganado (red) and Klagetoh (gray). Yei rugs depict the Holy People, and Yeibichai illustrate

Klagetoh rug design

© NATIONAL PARK SERVICE, IAN PIOCHE

is **Standing Cow Ruin,** where Navajo pictographs show a blue-and-white cow and a priest accompanying a Spanish cavalry unit.

The next turnoff is 18 miles from the visitors center. Take a right at the fork for **Mummy Cave Overlook,** named for two bodies found in the ruins that fill two caves, thought to be occupied between A.D. 300 and 1300. A right at the fork will bring you to **Massacre Cave Overlook.** When the Spanish sent Lieutenant Antonio de Narbona into the canyon in 1805 to quell Navajo raids, they found a group of women, children, and elders hiding there while the men were off hunting deer in the Lukachukai Mountains. In two days, Spanish riflemen killed 115 of the Navajo by bouncing bullets off the canyon ceiling from the rim above, and took 33 prisoners. The bones of the victims remain in the cave untouched, per Navajo custom.

South Rim Drive

Although not a through road, the South Rim Drive offers even more impressive views than the northern route. You'll pass the **Tunnel Overlook** and the **Tsegi Overlook** over the upper canyon before reaching the **Junction Overlook** where the Canyon del Muerto joins the Canyon de Chelly. **First Ruin** and **Junction Ruin** are both visible from here. Six miles from the visitors center is the turnoff for

ceremonies in which the Holy People are impersonated by human dancers. Prices range from the low hundreds to well into the thousands, with a quality 3-by-5-foot rug going for about $500-750. This is an exacting art, and, sadly, a dying one, since fewer young weavers are learning the old techniques. For this reason, a quality rug will hold its price well and probably even climb in value. Good rugs will also last for years – some old ones have endured over a century of boot traffic.

The Navajo originally learned the technique of **silversmithing** from Mexicans in the 1850s, before taking it to new levels. They don't have to melt down silver coins any more, but today's silver jewelry is just as impressive: chunky bracelets, elaborately detailed concha belts, rings and watchbands inlaid with turquoise and coral, and gorgeous squash-blossom necklaces that make your neck ache just to look at them. Silver jewelry is usually sand-cast and then polished to a bright luster, and die-stamped with decorative details. You'll often see Navajo matriarchs decked out in their best necklaces and bracelets, with enough turquoise to ransom a princess, and men wear the *ketoh*, (bow guard), a wide forearm band that is now purely decorative. Turquoise is the most common inlay material, but new techniques have seen the addition of gold and other precious minerals.

Navajo **sandpaintings** re-create the ceremonial designs drawn on hogan floors by medicine men, which are gathered and scattered to the winds when the ritual is finished. The paintings are drawn with glue on plywood or particleboard, then sprinkled with minerals gathered and ground on the reservation. Look for precise workmanship, and know that you're not getting a true religious artifact – small details are changed in the paintings to avoid offending the Holy People. Other types of **paintings** in oils and acrylics depict life on the reservation, and are sometimes quite abstract.

One of the most widely recognized type of basket made in the Southwest is the Navajo **ceremonial basket,** a wide, shallow dish woven of sumac and mahogany fibers. These are made using a concentric coil technique, and have geometric designs in muted colors. They're most commonly used in traditional weddings. Tribe members make many other types of crafts as well, including their own versions of Hopi **kachinas, wood carvings,** ceramic and alabaster **sculpture,** and **"folk art,"** a generic term for figurines carved from wood or fashioned from clay.

the **White House Overlook** which offers not only a great view but also the only way to reach the canyon bottom without a guide. The trail down to **White House Ruin,** dated to about A.D. 1200, is just over one mile from the canyon edge 500 feet down to the canyon floor and across it. The steep, rocky trail passes through a few short tunnels, a farm, and an orchard before crossing the stream in front of the well-preserved ruins (bring water). You'll find restrooms and Navajo artists selling jewelry nearby. Don't wander off the trail without a guide.

Farther down the rim drive is the turn-off for the overlook above **Sliding House Ruin** and the **Spider Rock Campground** (928/674-8261, www.spiderrockcamp ground.com). Owned by local Navajo resident Howard Smith (no relation), this place has tent sites for $12 and RV sites for $19, as well as solar-heated showers and two authentic hogans starting at $30. The South Rim Drive continues southeast as Route 7 (unpaved), but follow the pavement northeast back into the monument to the **Spider Rock Overlook,** the park's most outstanding viewing point. An 800-foot rock tower thrusts from the canyon bottom where three canyons come together. The monolith is understandably special to the Navajo, who call it Tse' Na' ashjé'ii and tell of the supernatural being who lives on top. Spider Woman teaches weaving on a loom whose warp is the rays of the sun. Navajo mothers once warned their children to behave or else Spider Woman would carry them to her perch, which is now white with bones.

Tours

Canyon De Chelly Unimog Tours (928/674-5433, www.canyondechellytours .com) offers tours of the canyon bottom in jeeps, the military-looking, natural-gas powered Unimog, or your own vehicle starting at $66 adults ($44 children) for half a day. They can also organize an overnight campout in the canyon. Authorized Navajo guides offers vehicle tours for $15 per hour, and hiking tours (15 people maximum) for the same price. Ask at the visitors center for details.

WHERE TO SHOP

There are two main options when it comes to purchasing indigenous crafts (well, three, if you count paying five times as much at a boutique back home): buy directly from the artists themselves, or buy from a trading post or gallery. Buying from the creator, either in his or her home or at a roadside or flea market stand, adds not only the personal touch but also the opportunity to get the best price. It helps to know what you're looking for in this situation, and to have an idea of how to judge quality and a fair price. To be honest, a good bit of the merchandise for sale at tourist spots like Monument Valley are, for lack of better words, cheap trinkets. This kind of stuff is relatively easy to spot, however.

Trading posts and galleries have higher prices, but at the better ones you can be assured that you're getting a quality product, with the reputation of the store behind it. Employees are happy to let you browse and to lend their expert advice if necessary, and can pack up and ship your purchases back home. Many also have pawn departments where people leave goods as collateral for cash loans and often don't return for them (dead pawn). Pawnshops are also common. This is a great way to get a deal on crafts, especially jewelry. Dead pawn is sometimes auctioned off on a monthly basis.

You'll find the best selection and quality at places like the **Tuba City Trading Post, Noteh Dineh** in Cortez, **Toh-Atin** in Durango, **Twin Rocks** in Bluff, **Fifth Generation** in Farmington, and **Blair's Dinnebito** in Page. For atmosphere, don't miss **Hatch Brothers** near Farmington, **Goulding's** and **Oljato** in Monument Valley, **Cow Canyon** in Bluff, and the **Hubbell Trading**

Chinle

There isn't much in the town of Chinle itself aside from a **Best Western** (928/674-5875), with 100 rooms for $90–110, and a **Holiday Inn** (928/674-5000, $90–130). Both have heated pools and restaurants open daily for all meals. The Chinle Comprehensive Health Care Facility is one of the best hospitals on the reservation, and combines traditional Navajo healing practices with modern medicine; it even includes a hogan for ceremonies. Look for labels in Navajo on products in Basha's Grocery Store, and for souvenirs try **Navajo Arts & Crafts Enterprises** at the main intersection.

Many Farms

North of Chinle at the intersection of Highways 59 and 191 is a settlement called Dá'ák'ehaláni by the Navajo. Several hundred small farms are cultivated in the area. The **Many Farms Inn** (928/781-6362, mfhsinn@manyfarms.bia.edu), behind the Many Farms High School, is run by Navajo students studying hotel management and tourism. Rooms in a school dormitory with shared bathrooms are $30 per night, and there's a TV lounge, a gym, and basketball courts.

HUBBELL TRADING POST NATIONAL HISTORIC SITE

The oldest continuously operating trading post on the Navajo Reservation was built on the bank of Ganado Wash in 1871. Clerk and interpreter John Lorenzo Hubbell bought the place seven years later, and it stayed in his family until the National Park Service took over in 1967. Hubbell quickly turned the post into one of the most successful in the Southwest, buying out and opening other posts throughout the Four Corners and earning the nickname "Don" Lorenzo, a Spanish term of respect, for his fair trading and hospitality.

A true friend of the Navajo, Hubbell spoke their language fluently and advised weavers on which designs would fetch the best prices. (The handsome Ganado pattern, with its deep red wool and cross motif, is still woven.) He brought a silversmith from Mexico to teach his

---

Post National Historic Site west of Window Rock. **Richardson's Trading Company** in Gallup can hold its own in both categories.

Wherever you buy a piece, try to find out where and when it was made, and ask for a **certificate of authenticity,** or else a receipt with the name and contact information of the artist or gallery, the artist's name and tribal affiliation, and the price, including the original price if you received a discount.

SHOPPING RESOURCES

Many trading posts and galleries have their own websites, that are continually updated as goods are bought and sold; these are listed in the various sections of this book. The **Southwest Indian Foundation** (505/863-4037, www.southwestindian.com) is a nonprofit organization with an extensive mail-order catalog of arts and crafts. Profits go to help native communities by supporting schools, providing food during holidays, and setting up homes for battered women. The nonprofit **Indian Arts and Crafts Association** (505/265-9149, www.iaca.com) offers consumer tips and lots of other information on their website.

The **Indian Arts and Crafts Act of 1990** prohibits the misrepresentation of Native American arts and crafts (defined as a tribe member or artisan certified by a tribe) produced after 1935. For more information, contact the Indian Arts & Crafts Board of the U.S. Department of the Interior (888/ART-FAKE, 202/208-3773, www.doi.gov/iacb).

The Southwest Parks and Monuments Association puts out the pocket-size *A Guide to Navajo Rugs,* available at many bookstores and gift shops in the Four Corners.

art, and treated Navajo struck down by small-pox. The Hubbells—Lorenzo, his wife Una Rubi, and their four children—amassed one of the largest art collections in the Southwest in their home next to the post.

Today the original 160-acre homestead, one mile west of Ganado on Highway 264, is administered by the National Park Service (928/755-3475, www.nps.gov/hutr, 8 A.M.–6 P.M. daily, until 5 P.M. in winter, free). The old trading post is run by the Western National Parks Association (www.spma.org). They still buy and sell crafts, food, and supplies, though most sales now are to tourists, and stock a king's ransom in Navajo rugs in the rug room. Demonstrations and auctions of Native American crafts are held throughout the year, and daily tours take visitors into the Hubbell home ($2 pp), which retains all its original furnishings, except for the rugs. The ceiling in the main hallway is covered with dozens of woven baskets, and works by artists who visited the family adorn the walls, including many of E. A. Burbank's portraits, mostly of Native Americans, done with red conte crayon.

Hopi Reservation

A cultural island within the larger Navajo Reservation, the Hopi Reservation centers around 12 ancient villages on three fingerlike mesas that rise to 7,200 feet. First, Second, and Third Mesa were named from east to west, since early explorers arrived from the east, and are strung together by Highway 264 between Tuba City and Ganado. A few of the Hopi villages have been inhabited for over eight centuries. This is a quiet, isolated place, whose main draw is the almost tangible sense of tradition that hangs in the clear air.

The boundaries of the Hopis' ancestral lands, or Tutsqua, extended from Canyon de Chelly and the Four Corners to the San Francisco Peaks, and from Navajo Mountain to the Zuni Reservation near Gallup. The 600-foot-high Hopi mesas are dotted with homes made from adobe, cinder block, and stone, standing alongside trailers, pickup trucks, and the shells of unfinished or abandoned buildings. Ladders poke out of kivas, both above and below ground level, and scattered outhouses indicate which of the traditional villages do not have plumbing. Most of the Hopi are farmers or artisans and highly respectful of tradition, although more and more live in modern towns in between the older villages perched atop the steep-walled mesas.

The Hopi welcome visitors; they just expect you to behave yourself. The tribe guards its privacy and traditions even more than the Navajo, so photography, videotaping, sketching, and any other methods of recording are *strictly* prohibited—no exceptions. Accept the fact that this is one part of your vacation you'll have to recall from memory, because if you're caught breaking this rule, you will be asked to leave.

Most social dances are open to non-Hopi—some require a personal invitation from a tribe member—but many kachina dances and all snake dances and flute ceremonies are closed to visitors. If you want to watch a ceremony, be aware that you will be considered a part of the collective spiritual effort, so you should act and dress respectfully. This means no shorts, short skirts, or T-shirts, no loud talking, and no striding across the plaza to get a closer look at someone's headdress. Many residents sell crafts and food from their homes, and advertise with signs out front—try some traditional, wafer-thin *piiki* bread, made with blue-corn flour. Don't wander far down back alleys, though, particularly during ceremonies, and get permission from a village leader if you plan on spending more than a few hours in any village.

Visitors are prohibited from certain culturally sensitive areas on the reservation; check with the Hopi Cultural Center on Second Mesa for a list of these sites, and a schedule

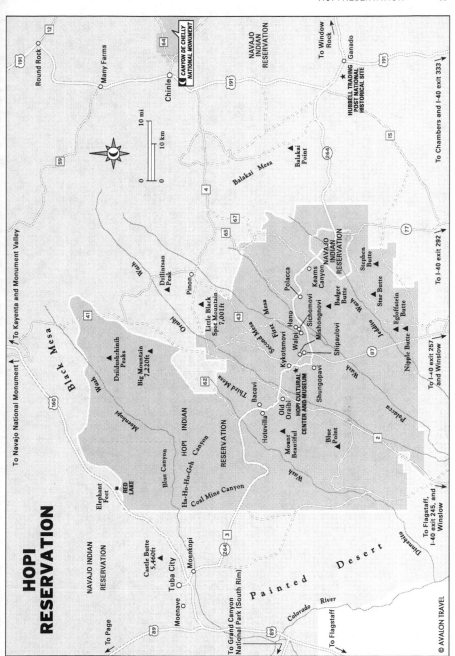

HOPI RESERVATION

NAVAJO INDIAN RESERVATION

To Page

To Navajo National Monument

To Kayenta and Monument Valley

Round Rock

Many Farms

Chinle

CANYON DE CHELLY NATIONAL MONUMENT

NAVAJO INDIAN RESERVATION

To Window Rock

Ganado

HUBBELL TRADING POST NATIONAL HISTORICAL SITE

To Chambers and I-40 exit 333

Balakai Mesa

Balakai Point

10 mi

10 km

Black Mesa

Oraibi Wash

Drilintsan Peak

Pinon

Little Black Spot Mountain 7,001ft

Dziitushchinih Peaks

Big Mountain 7,220ft

First Mesa

Second Mesa

Polacca

Keams Canyon

Sichomovi

Hano

Walpi

Mishongnovi

Shipaulovi

Badger Butte

Stephen Butte

Star Butte

Egloffstein Butte

Nipple Butte

To I-40 exit 292

To Window Rock

Kykotsmovi

HOPI CULTURAL CENTER AND MUSEUM

Shungopavi

Shongopavi

To I-40 exit 257 and Winslow

HOPI INDIAN RESERVATION

Third Mesa

Bacavi

Old Oraibi

Hotevilla

Mount Beautiful

Blue Point

Moenkopi Wash

Blue Canyon

Ha-Ho-Ho-Geh Canyon

Coal Mine Canyon

Elephant Feet

RED LAKE

Castle Butte 5,460ft

Tuba City

Moenave

To Grand Canyon National Park (South Rim)

Colorado River

To Flagstaff

Painted Desert

Dinnebito Wash

To Flagstaff, I-40 exit 245, and Winslow

© AVALON TRAVEL

of religious ceremonies open to the public. A number of tribal members offer guided cultural and archaeological tours of the area. Try **Gary Tso** (928/734-2567, lhhunter58@hotmail .com) or **Bertram Tsavadawa** (928/734-9544 or 928/306-7849, ancientpathways2004@ yahoo.com). Professional anthropologist

Micah Loma'omvaya (928/734-0230 or 928/734-9549, info@hopitours.com or hopian-thro@yahoo.com) offers archaeological tours to ruins and other sites on the reservation, starting at $75 per person for a half day.

The information in this section is listed from east to west, following Highway 264 from Ganado to Tuba City.

HOPI CRAFTS

The Peaceful People are best known for two types of crafts. Hopi **silver jewelry** is more delicate than the Navajo style, and dates to the 1890s, when Sikyatala, the first Hopi silversmith, learned his craft from artisans at the Zuñi pueblo. Since World War II it has been done in an overlay style, in which a design is cut from a flat sheet of silver and set in front of another sheet that has been textured and oxidized until black. Hopi jewelry is marked with the artist's name, clan, or village, and the design may be pictorial or abstract. Gold and inlaid precious stones are sometimes incorporated into the design, which range from rings, bracelets, and bolo tie clasps to necklaces, belt buckles, and button covers.

Kachina (katsina) dolls were originally used to teach children about the spirit beings who live in the San Francisco Peaks and bring rain. These brightly painted figures are carved from the root of the cottonwood with an attached base, and can be amazingly detailed. They come in all sizes, and the quality of the carving and painting varies as widely as the price. Prime examples are true works of art, and justifiably fetch thousands of dollars. There are dozens of kachinas depicted as dolls, including Mongwa, the Great Horned Owl; Salako Mana and Salaka Taka, the male and female kachina leaders; and the humorous Koyemsi and Koshare clowns. Kachinas are some of the most distinctive souvenirs of the Southwest, and if they strike your fancy, it's well worth it to read up on the art and talk to carvers.

Hopi artisans also make **baskets** and **paintings** not too unlike those of the Navajo, as well as ground-fired **pottery.**

EAST OF FIRST MESA

The natural oasis of **Keams Canyon,** called Pongsikya by the Hopi, was originally known to Anglo settlers as Peach Orchard Springs. Englishman Thomas Keam, once a trooper under Colonel Kit Carson (whose own 1863 signature is inscribed in the canyon wall), opened a trading post here in 1869. Keams married a Hopi woman and quarreled strongly with the Bureau of Indian Affairs (BIA) superintendent, who demanded that the Hopi stop their ceremonial dances and send their children to the nearby BIA boarding school under threat of force. The superintendent was eventually dismissed.

Today, Keams Canyon is a U.S. government town with a hospital, post office, and **Keam's Canyon Shopping Center. McGee's Indian Art Gallery** (928/738-2295, www.hopiart .com) is inside, centered around Keam's original trading post, and selling an excellent selection of local crafts, particularly kachinas. They have added a grocery store, a coin laundry, and a small café. They also offer lodgings; call for details. Follow the road up Keams Wash 1.5 miles to a shelter on the west (left), marking an inscription left by Kit Carson.

At the southern tip of Antelope Mesa are the ruins of **Awat'ovi** (ah-WAHT-oh-vee), which has a sad and bloody history. A Franciscan church built in this Hopi village in 1629 was destroyed by the tribe and residents of other pueblos who feared the friars' influence. When Awat'ovi's residents allowed the missionaries back in two decades later, however, the other Hopi villages took drastic steps. Almost all of the village's men were killed, and its women and children scattered among other villages. The area is closed to the public.

FIRST MESA

At the base of First Mesa is **Polacca** (po-LAH-kah), founded in 1890 by a resident of Hano. The BIA tried to convince Hopi in the older villages up above to move here, but to this day most of Polacca's residents still consider themselves to be from Walpi or Sichomovi. In Polacca is the turnoff for the road to the top of First Mesa, a steep and narrow paved road just over a mile long. (Larger vehicles must be parked at the bottom.)

The first traditional village on the mesa is **Hano,** which was founded by Tewa Indians from the Rio Grande near Albuquerque. Fleeing the Spanish after the Pueblo Revolt of 1680, the Tewa were allowed to settle here by the Hopi if they agreed to guard access to the mesa. This was the home of the famous Hopi potter Nampeyo, born in 1860, who based her work on the ancient techniques used in pottery shards dug up by anthropologists. Thanks to the efforts of Fred Harvey, who had her display her work at the Grand Canyon, she eventually became famous and traveled around the country demonstrating her craft. She eventually became blind, but was able to teach her daughters her techniques. Her legacy continues in various homes selling pottery; look for signs.

Sichomovi (see-CHO-mo-vi), just beyond Hano, was founded in 1750 by residents of **Walpi** (WAHL-pee), which perches on the narrow southernmost tip of the mesa. Walpi, meaning "the gap," refers to the narrow neck of stone that isolates the tiny village almost completely from the rest of the mesa—and, it seems, from the modern age as well. Walpi lacks running water and electricity, and is exceedingly traditional. Along with its setting, the village is known for its crafts and its ceremonies, which are unfortunately closed to the public. With nothing but sky and stone in every direction, Walpi offers a striking panorama that has hardly changed in centuries. Arrange a guided walking tour (928/737-2262 or 928/737-2670, $8 pp) in Sichomovi, or else contact the village of Walpi directly, ideally in advance (928/737-9556).

Walpi sits above the original settlement of Old Walpi, which was inhabited since the 13th century and abandoned for this more secure location after the Pueblo Revolt. The ruins of an old Spanish mission are also visible (although closed to visitors), as are prehistoric foot trails up the mesa and stone depressions used to catch rainwater.

SECOND MESA

Highway 264 is joined by Highway 87 at the foot of Second Mesa. Near the intersection are a **post office,** the **Sekakuku supermarket,** offering deli takeout food, and **LKD's Diner,** serving a small menu for breakfast and lunch Monday–Saturday in season; Monday–Friday otherwise. Al Sakakuku's **Hopi Fine Arts** has a good selection of crafts.

Villages

Two routes take Highway 264 to the top of Second Mesa. They split half a mile west of the Highway 87 intersection, where you'll find a **gas station** and the **Honani Crafts Gallery** (928/737-2238), which has an excellent array of jewelry behind four stained-glass windows depicting kachinas. From here, a steep, twisting track—more of a loading ramp than a road—leads up to two traditional villages. **Shipaulovi** (shih-PAW-loh-vee) has little more than an old abandoned trading post and a few homes. The name means "place of the mosquitoes." **Mishongnovi** (mi-SHONG-no-vee) is at the very top of mesa, with not a yard to spare between the building walls and the cliff edges.

The other route takes you past the turnoff for **Shungopavi** (shon-GO-pah-vee), meaning "sand grass spring place." Its story is similar to Walpi—an older village at the base of the mesa was abandoned for a more secure spot after the Pueblo Revolt. A number of galleries sell jewelry and other crafts, and you can grab a bite here at HildaBurger.

Hopi Cultural Center and Vicinity

This small complex (928/734-2401, www .hopiculturalcenter.com) serves as unofficial nexus of the reservation where the two routes rejoin on top of Second Mesa. It has a museum of Hopi crafts and cultural items (928/734-6650, 8 A.M.–5 P.M. Mon.–Fri., 9 A.M.–3 P.M. Sat. and Sun., $3 pp), as well as a motel with modest but clean rooms for $95–100 ($70–75 Oct.–Mar.) and a campground. A restaurant serves dishes ($5–9) such as burgers, blue-corn pancakes, and *nöqkwivi*, a traditional hominy-and-mutton stew for all meals daily. The **Hopi Arts and Crafts Silver Cooperative Guild** (866/718-8476, www.hopiarts-craftsco-op.com, 8 A.M.–6 P.M. Mon.–Fri., 9 A.M.–4:30 P.M. Sat. and Sun.), established in 1949, is nearby in a two-story pink building. They stock a large selection of handmade jewelry and other crafts. Many trainees have gone on to start their own successful businesses.

A mostly dirt road (Highway 43) leaves from here north up Second Mesa, joining Highway 41 at Piñon, offering a scenic alternate way to reach Chinle and Canyon de Chelly. Other galleries are scattered along the roads on Second Mesa, including **Sewukiwma's Arts & Crafts** (928/734-0388) and Alph Secakuku's **Hopi Fine Arts** (Hwys. 264 and 87, 928/737-2222). One and a half miles east of the cultural center is Janice and Joseph Day's **Tsakurshovi**

(928/734-2478), a fascinating store with a great selection of Hopi and Navajo work, including jewelry, kachinas, and baskets. The Days supply the Hopi with materials for their ceremonies, which explains all the turtle shells, furs, and herbs around, and are a font of information on the area.

THIRD MESA

Kykotsmovi (kee-KOOTS-moh-vee) was founded by residents of Old Oraibi near a spring at the base of Third Mesa. Today it's surrounded by fruit trees and is the home of the modern Hopi government. The **Hopi Cultural Preservation Office** (928/734-3612 or 928/734-3000) provides visitor information out of the Tribal Headquarters building, and the **Kykotsmovi Village Store** offers sandwiches, pizzas, and other deli items. Highway 2 heads south from here for I-15 at the town of Leupp (LOOP). This is the quickest way back to Flagstaff, and is a lovely, empty drive that's paved the entire way.

On the way up onto Third Mesa to Old Oraibi you'll pass **Pumpkin Seed Point,** a picnic area with a great view of the Hopi

© JULIAN SMITH

The Hopi Mesa seems little changed in decades, if not centuries.

buttes to the south. Soon comes the turnoff for Old Oraibi, two miles west of Kykotsmovi, where you'll find the pink **Monongya Gallery** (928/734-2344), with a large selection of paintings, jewelry, pottery, and baskets made by various tribes. Their selection of kachinas is one of the largest around.

Inhabited since the mid 12th century, **Old Oraibi** (oh-RYE-bee) is arguably the oldest continually occupied community in the country. In 1906, this windswept collection of stone and cinder-block buildings was split by internal strife. The Bear clan, led by Tawaquaptewa, wanted to cooperate with the U.S. government's Indian Service, while the Skeleton clan, led by Youkeoma, refused. They settled the dispute with a pushing contest: A line was etched in the ground and the groups lined up on either side, with their respective leaders in front. At a signal each started shoving. When the dust cleared Tawaquaptewa's clan had won. Youkeoma led his people off to found Hotevilla, where they were labeled "hostiles" by the U.S. government. The event is commemorated by an inscription in the mesa, near the line itself, which reads:

Well it have to be this way not
pass me over this LINE
it will be DONE.
Sept. 8, 1906.

Wandering the streets of Old Oraibi is an experience in time travel. Notice the ruins of the old Mennonite church at the south end of the mesa, built in 1901 and destroyed by lightning (a second strike) in 1942, to the quiet delight of many of the town's traditional residents. A few homes sell crafts.

A few miles west on Highway 264 are the villages of **Hotevilla** (HOAT-vih-lah), founded by Youkeoma's people, and **Bacavi** (BAH-kah-vee), founded three years later by another Oraibi splinter group. These are residential villages without much to see.

West of Third Mesa

Just over 30 miles west of Bacavi and Hotevilla is **Coal Mine Canyon,** a marvelous ravine that leads north to join Blue Canyon and, eventually, Moenkopi Wash toward Tuba City. Look for a dirt road between mile markers 336 and 337 leading to a windmill, beside the rodeo grounds. The Navajo call this serrated landscape *hááhonoojí,* or "jagged," and the Hopi tell of Quayowuuti, the Eagle Woman from Old Oraibi, who stepped from the edge of the canyon to her death. Her ghost is said to appear under the full moon.

Just east of Tuba City on Highway 264 is the town of **Moenkopi** (a small cultural island separated from the greater Hopi Reservation. "The place of running water" was founded in the 1870s by farmers from Oraibi, who would run to their fields and back—a distance of over 30 miles—several times a week. Like many Hopi villages, it is split into upper and lower sections.

East of Flagstaff

I-40 leaves the San Francisco Mountains for the high desert plains as it rolls east toward New Mexico. It follows the Little Colorado River upstream from Winslow to Holbrook, where it is joined by the Rio Puerco. Rugged hills dotted with buttes and junipers continue past the Petrified Forest and Painted Desert to the southern end of the Defiance Plateau at the state line.

METEOR CRATER

About 50,000 years ago, a meteorite 150 feet across slammed into the Arizona plain at upwards of 30,000 mph, igniting an explosion greater than 20 million tons of TNT. The impact threw 175 million tons of stone into the atmosphere, uplifted the bedrock by 150 feet, and turned graphite into diamond at pressures of over 20 million pounds per square inch—and it left a really, *really* big hole in the ground. You can fit 20 football fields into the crater, which is 2.5 miles in circumference and deeper than the Washington Monument. It was originally thought to be volcanic in origin, but the tireless research of Philadelphia mining engineer Daniel Barringer convinced the world otherwise, even though his efforts to find the meteorite itself didn't pan out.

The crater (800/289-5898 or 928/289-5898, www.meteorcrater.com, 7 A.M.–7 P.M. daily, 8 A.M.–5 P.M. Labor Day–Memorial Day, $15 adults, $7 children) is five miles south of I-40 exit 233. The "first proved and best preserved meteorite crater in the world" is privately owned, and has a well-done museum on its edge with exhibits on astrogeology and space travel. A computer simulation of a meteor impact offers the perverse pleasure of seeing how big and fast you can make your imaginary comet before it vaporizes the earth. There's a gift shop and snack bar, and guided walks a third of a mile around the rim trail are included in admission. On the crater floor, a dummy figure in a space suit provides a sense of scale; Apollo astronauts trained here before going to the moon. On the way there from the interstate you'll pass the **Meteor Crater RV Park** (800/478-4002) with 81 sites ($24–26), a gas station, showers, and laundry.

WINSLOW

This city was founded in 1882 as a railroad stop near Sunset Crossing, one of the few places to ford the sandy-bottomed Little Colorado River. Winslow hit its stride in the early 1900s, when cross-country traffic poured in off the new Route 66 and local ranchers shipped their stock out through the rail terminal. Fred Harvey opened La Posada, perhaps the prettiest of his Spanish-style hotels, and in 1930, Charles Lindberg flew to Winslow Airport, which he had designed as a stop between Chicago and Los Angeles.

The town slid toward the end of the 20th century, when traffic began to pass by on both the interstate and the railroad. Still, you've probably heard of Winslow if you've ever listened to pop radio: The Eagles sang about "standing on a corner in Winslow, Arizona" in their hit "Take It Easy." Today, Winslow (pop. 9,500) has a south-of-the-border ambience, with lots of weathered adobe buildings. It's hoped that the restoration of La Posada will inject some much-needed vitality into the town, which has a number of interesting sights within day-trip distance.

The **Winslow Chamber of Commerce** (101 E. Second St., 928/289-2434, www.winslow arizona.org, 8 A.M.–5 P.M. Mon.–Fri.) can answer more questions about the city. If you're here in October, don't miss the **"Standin' On the Corner" Festival,** with music, arts, crafts, an auction, and a car show.

Sights

The actual corner that Jackson Browne and Glen Frey sang about is commemorated at the **Standin' on the Corner Park** at 2nd Street (Route 66) and Kinsley Avenue. You can have your photo taken next to the statue of one of the Eagles holding a guitar, or the "girl, my Lord, in a flatbed Ford" painted in a two-story mural on the facing wall. This part of downtown is starting to cash in on its Route 66 heritage, with shops offering souvenirs and memorabilia.

The quirky **Old Trails Museum** (212 Kinsley St., 928/289-5861, 10 A.M.–4P.M. Tues.–Sat., free) is housed in a 1921 bank building, nicknamed "Winslow's attic." An interesting collection includes dinosaur bones, Route 66 memorabilia, Anasazi artifacts, and the still of a local moonshiner, who lived to the age of 97 on a daily breakfast of black coffee, raw eggs, and a shot of his own firewater.

North of Winslow on the banks of the Little Colorado River is **Homolovi Ruins State Park** (928/289-4106, http://azstateparks .com, 8 A.M.–5 P.M. daily, $5 per car), opened in 1993. The site's four main pueblo ruins were inhabited in the 13th and 14th centuries by the ancestors of the Hopi, who eventually migrated north to the three Hopi mesas. Their name for the group archaeologists call the Anasazi (or today, the Ancestral Puebloans) is the Hisat'sinom, and the Hopi still consider this part of the ancestral homeland and make periodic pilgrimages. More than 300 archaeological sites have been uncovered here, and three of the four pueblos are open to the public. There's a visitors center and a 53-site campground ($12–19). To get there, take I-40 exit 257 to Highway 87, go north 1.3 miles to the entrance on the left, then proceed another two miles to the visitors center.

For a break from the high-desert heat, head to **Clear Creek,** where you can swim, boat, or fish. (Bring a canoe or kayak and paddle into deep, rocky Clear Creak Canyon.) Free camping is available at McHood Park (928/289-5714), five miles from town. Take Route 87 south to Highway 99 and turn left.

Shopping

Roadworks Gifts & Souvenirs (101 W. 2nd St., 928/289-5423) is on the 2nd floor overlooking the Corner Park. They stock every kind of Route 66 souvenir you can think of, plus a few hundred more: T-shirts, bumper stickers, books, magnets, postcards, and mugs. Don't miss Bob Waldemire's postcards and map-guide to Route 66. He used to run the Route 66 visitors center in Seligman, west of Flagstaff, and his detailed drawings are works of art.

Accommodations and Food

Architect Mary Coulter designed **(La Posada** (303 E. 2nd St., 928/289-4366, www .laposada.org, $100) for hotelier Fred Harvey in 1930, calling it her masterpiece. Built in the style of an old Spanish hacienda, the "Last Great Railroad Hotel" counted among its guests luminaries such as Albert Einstein, Howard Hughes, Dorothy Lamour, and the Crown Prince of Japan. All trains between Chicago and Los Angeles stopped here, as did planes before better designs let them make the trip without stopping. It was closed for 40 years and nearly razed before it was rescued from the wrecking ball in the late 1990s and put on the historical preservation list.

Somewhere, Mary Coulter is smiling. Thanks to the tireless efforts of owner Allan Affeldt and his wife, artist Tina Mion, the hotel is well on its way to recapturing its former glory. Suits of armor, religious icons, and Tina's large, intriguing paintings make up an eclectic art collection, and Amtrak trains still rumble past the cottonwoods and gardens out back. Decorated with Navajo rugs and artwork, the **(Turquoise Room Restaurant** (928/289-2888, all meals daily) serves wonderful contemporary Southwest cuisine including recipes from the Harvey heyday of the 1930s. Dishes ($18–30 for dinner) use local ingredients such as lamb and Colorado elk, and go well with a chili-pepper martini or prickly-pear cactus bread pudding for dessert. On either side of the restaurant are a martini lounge and the gift shop. This is a special place, well worth a stop if only for lunch.

Winslow has many inexpensive hotels, including a **Motel 6** (520 W. Desmond St., 928/289-9581, $50–75) and an **Econo Lodge** (1706 N. Park Dr., 928/289-4687, $50–100). The **Comfort Inn** (1701 N. Park Dr., 928/289-4638, $80–100) has the family-oriented Adobe Inn restaurant (dinner Mon.–Sat., entrées $8–18) and a heated outdoor pool.

Family-owned for half a century, the **Casa Blanca Cafe** (1201 E. 2nd St., 928/289-4191, lunch and dinner daily) serves up authentic Mexican food every day of the week. Entrées are $5–10. Grab a burger or burrito at **BoJo's Grill & Sports Club** (117 W. 2nd St. 928/289-0616, lunch and dinner daily) and settle down to watch the Arizona Diamondbacks play.

Transportation

Amtrak serves Winslow, but the station (next to La Posada on East 2nd St.) is unstaffed; call 800/872-7245 for information. **Greyhound** buses stop at the Super American Truck Stop (2201 N. Park Dr., 928/289-2171).

HOLBROOK

This ranching center was founded, as so many other southwestern cities were, with the arrival of the railroad in 1881. The second-largest ranch in the county, the Hashknife, was based nearby, where cowboys herded up to 60,000 cows and 2,000 horses across two million acres. This attracted rustlers, naturally, and for a time Holbrook was known as the "town too tough for women and children." Patrons at the Bucket of Blood Saloon tried to outdo each other in downing shots of whiskey "before they touched the bottom of the glass," and cowboys would gallop through town on payday with guns blazing, crying "Hide out, kids, the cowboys are in town!" In 1887, Sheriff Perry Owens (scoffed at on arrival as a bit of a dandy) single-handedly killed three members of the Cooper-Blevins gang in a gunfight, and wounded a fourth. Until 1914, Holbrook was known as the only county seat in the country without a church.

Today Holbrook (pop. 5,000) has the easiest access to the Petrified Forest National Park, and provides a rest stop along I-40.

Sights

Holbrook's 1898 county courthouse has been turned into the **Navajo County Museum** (100 E. Arizona St., 8 A.M.–5 P.M. daily, free), full to the rafters with local history. The collection focuses on Holbrook's colorful Wild West past, and the claustrophobic jail downstairs is decorated with prisoners' graffiti. Native American dances are held here on weekdays in the summer. The offices of the **Holbrook Chamber of Commerce** (928/524-6558 or 800/524-2459) are here as well.

Entertainment and Events

If you happen to arrive in Holbrook right after the holidays and have someone in Scottsdale you want to write to, you're in luck. Reenactors with the **Hashknife Pony Express** carry mail on horseback along the old express route every January. (Send your mail, marked "Via Pony Express" in the lower-left-hand corner, enclosed in another envelope addressed to Postmaster, Holbrook, AZ, 86025.) Holbrook's **Old West Days** in August bring more reenactors, music, crafts, dancing, and bike and foot races. In September, the **Navajo County Fair** arrives, and the **Christmas Parade of Lights** illuminates downtown the first Saturday in December.

Shopping

With all the petrified wood for sale in town, it's hard to believe there's any left in the park—but luckily the law dictates that anything offered for sale must be taken from private land. Polished specimens, geodes, turquoise, and other geological curiosities are offered at places like the **Rainbow Rock Shop** (101 Navajo Blvd., 928/524-2384), with huge green dinosaurs guarding its entrance near the train tracks.

Accommodations and Food

Fittingly, Hopi Drive and Navajo Boulevard are Holbrook's main commercial arteries, and are where you'll find most of the city's hotels and restaurants. Leading the least-expensive category by a wide margin is the **◖ Wigwam Motel** (811 W. Hopi Dr., 928/524-3048, www.wigwam-motel-arizona.com, $48–54). It looks like a classic car collection parked among a forest of big fake tepees, and that's just what it is. It was built in the 1940s, and the wigwams still have their original furniture and all their Route

classic cars and imitation teepee hotel rooms at Holbrook's Wigwam Motel

© JULIAN SMITH

66 charm. Another option around $50 is the **American Best Inn** (2211 E. Navajo Blvd., 928/524-2654).

In the $50–100 category is the **Days Inn** (2601 Navajo Blvd., 928/524-6949), and rooms at the **Best Western Arizonian Inn** (2508 Navajo Blvd., 928/524-2611) are $85–115. The **OK RV Park** (1576 Roadrunner Rd., 928/524-3226) has 136 sites for $14–34. There's also a **KOA Kampground** (102 Hermosa Dr., 928/524-6689, $23–29) with 208 sites, plus all the usual KOA amenities.

Authentic diner fare befitting Holbrook's location on Old Route 66 is what makes **Joe & Aggie's Cafe** (120 W. Hopi Dr., 928/524-6540, all meals Mon.–Sat.) such a gem. From the honey bottles for the sopapillas to the cheesy joke books and chicken-fried steak platters, Holbrook's oldest restaurant (1946) does Mexican and American road food right. Sandwiches are $4–5, entrées $6–8, and breakfasts $4–7. They also cut hair. For steaks head to the Western-themed **Butterfield Stage Co. Steak House** (609 W. Hopi Dr., 928/524-3447, dinner daily), and for Italian food try the **Mesa Italiana** (2318 E. Navajo Blvd., 928/524-6696, dinner daily), where traditional Mediterranean dishes are around $8 for lunch and $9–17 for dinner.

Transportation

The town **Greyhound** stop (928/524-3832) is at the Circle K at 101 Mission Lane and Navajo Boulevard.

PETRIFIED FOREST NATIONAL PARK

This park, extending both north and south of the interstate, protects one of the world's largest and most colorful concentrations of petrified wood. The petrifaction process was so exact that in some trees the original cell structure is still clearly visible. A wealth of late Triassic fossils and ruins and petroglyphs from 10,000 years of human habitation complete the picture. The area was declared a national monument by President Theodore Roosevelt in 1906, and in 1962 it was designated a national park.

In the late Triassic Period, over 200 million years ago, this part of Arizona crawled with giant reptiles and fish-eating amphibians. Some of the first dinosaurs plodded among cycads, ferns, and early conifers. Huge trees, some up to 200 feet high, were uprooted by wind or old age and swept down into a vast floodplain and buried in silt and mud. Over time, silica-bearing groundwater seeped through the wood and replaced it, cell by cell, with silica. Different minerals tinted the silica a rainbow of brilliant colors. Erosion eventually exposed the fossilized logs in the hillsides of the Painted Desert. Native legends regarding the logs' origins are even more colorful: the Navajo considered the logs to be the bones of the giant Yeitso, killed by the Hero Twins, while the Paiute told how they were the arrow shafts of the god Shuav.

THE PAINTED DESERT

The Navajo call it *halchíítah*, meaning "among the colors." The arid badlands of the late-Triassic Chinle Formation are famous for their psychedelic scenery, heavily eroded and dotted with buttes and mesas of nearly every color imaginable. Pastel pinks, reds, yellows, greens, and grays stain the barren hillsides, and crazy eroded shapes make up a surrealist landscape that is almost unbelievable at sunrise and sunset.

The Painted Desert extends in a narrow arc for about 160 miles from Cameron to the Petrified Forest, between the Little Colorado River and the Hopi tablelands. Most of the soils were laid down as silt and volcanic ash, and are marked by clays that shrink and swell so much as they get wet and dry that hardly anything can grow. A few different factors have dictated which colors ended up where. Reds, oranges, and pinks come from iron and aluminum oxides concentrated in slowly deposited sediments, while blues, grays, and purples are the results of rapid events, such as floods, that removed oxygen from the soils.

Visiting the Park

A 28-mile drive is the park's backbone, arcing from I-40 exit 311 to Highway 180 east of Holbrook. Everything is on or near this road, which connects to seven short trails. Very few people venture off it, but backcountry camping is permitted (with a free permit) in the psychedelic Petrified Forest National Desert Wilderness Area north of the interstate and near the Rainbow Forest area in the south end of the park.

Warnings against stealing petrified wood are everywhere, but some people still do it, even though there is plenty for sale in Holbrook gathered from private lands (and thus legal). "Conscience wood" displays showcase pieces that guilt-ridden visitors have returned after taking them home, often after a rash of mysteriously bad luck.

Starting at the northern end, the **Painted Desert Visitor Center** (928/524-6228, www.nps.gov/pefo, 8 A.M.–5 P.M. daily, 7 A.M.–7 P.M. in summer, $10 per vehicle) has an introductory video, bookstore, restrooms, and general information on the park. A short distance farther, past viewing points over the Painted Desert, is the **Painted Desert Inn** (8 A.M.–5 P.M. daily), a National Historic Landmark decorated inside with a handpainted skylight, punched tin fixtures by the CCC, and murals by Hopi artist Fred Kabotie. There are cultural demonstrations here during the summer, and rangers lead tours year-round.

Keep going past more viewing points and cross the interstate (no access) and the train tracks to reach the central portion of the park, where one of the prehistoric ruins and many of the petroglyphs are found at **Puerco Pueblo** ruins and **Newspaper Rock.** (The pueblo is believed to have been occupied twice, A.D. 1100–1200 and 1300–1400) **The Tepees** are actually rock formations. A short side road leads to **Blue Mesa,** with panoramic viewing points and a mile-long interpretive loop trail. Farther down the main road, **Agate Bridge** is a large petrified log spanning an eroded gully.

The southern part of the park is where you'll find the best petrified stone wood. A trail starting near the Rainbow Forest Museum leads to the popular **Long Logs Trail** and **Agate House,** an eight-room structure built by ancient inhabitants entirely out of petrified wood, which has been partially restored. The **Rainbow Forest Museum** (8 A.M.–5 P.M. daily, extended hours in summer) displays astounding fossils near a bookstore and information desk. Out back is the short **Giant Logs Trail,** true to its name—one stone trunk is nearly 10 feet across at the base. Across the road, **Fred Harvey's Curios and Fountain** sells souvenirs and snacks.

Just outside the scenic drive's southern entrance are two places not affiliated with the park: the **Petrified Forest Museum Gift Shop** (928/524-3470) and the **Crystal Forest Museum and Gift Shop** (928/524-3500). Both let you satisfy your acquisitive cravings with beautiful petrified wood for sale, and allow camping on their property.

Gallup and Vicinity

Although it's outside the reservation boundary, Gallup (pop. 20,000) is the Navajo Nation's most important commercial center. A plethora of arts-and-crafts shops and galleries, along with a good slice of turn-of-the-20th-century history and the country's premiere Native American gathering, await those who look past the city's weather-beaten facade. Surrounded by the Navajo and Zuni Reservations (and within an hour of the Acoma, Laguna, and Jicarilla Apache Reservations), unpretentious Gallup easily earns the title Gateway to Indian Country.

History

Coal was discovered in the area near the middle of the 19th century, helping to insure that the Atlantic & Pacific Railroad chose a route that passed near this tiny stagecoach stop. The town itself was founded in 1881, named after a railroad paymaster, and quickly became a timber- and coal-mining hub. Between 1880 and 1948, more than 50 mines were in operation near Gallup, which stayed relatively quiet as Western cities went. In 1929 alone, 25,177 railroad cars full of coal left the city's freight station, averaging one 70-car train every day of the year. The coal boom drew people from around the world to Gallup's already diverse ethnic mix, which included members of the Navajo and Hopi tribes and the Acoma and Zuni Pueblos. Workers from Germany, Italy, Spain, Greece, China, Japan, Austria, Wales, Scotland, and Yugoslavia, among other countries, left descendents who still call the city home.

Gallup Today

A 30-car coal train still rumbles of out Gallup seven days a week, and the Santa Fe Railroad passes through town every 15 minutes, but the city has shifted its focus to tourism, particularly the rich arts-and-crafts traditions of the nearby Native American tribes. Making Gallup "Indian Capital of the World" has been a successful marketing strategy; the city now boasts more than 100 trading posts, shops, and galleries, along with a few good museums and some 2,000 hotel and motel rooms for the traffic from I-40.

A classic, neon-signed stretch of Old Route 66 serves as Gallup's Main Street, parallel to the train tracks. The 12-block downtown area, enclosed by Main Street, Hill Avenue, 1st Street, and 4th Street, contains most of Gallup's galleries and trading posts, along with a reassuring amount of public artwork, including a mural on the Navajo code talkers on 2nd Street near Main Street. Motels and restaurants (mostly serving Mexican food) line Route 66/Main Street toward either end of town. Gritty pawnshops sidle up next to high-end craft boutiques, and Navajo cowboys share the sidewalks with tourists hopping off the interstate for a quick browse.

The scourge of drunk driving reaches a pinnacle in Gallup, so keep a sharp eye out behind the wheel, especially on weekend nights.

Sights

The 1916 Santa Fe Train Depot in the center of town was renovated in 1995 and turned into the **Gallup Cultural Center** (201 E. Hwy. 66, 505/863-4131, 8 A.M.–4 P.M. Mon.–Fri.,

THE CROWNPOINT RUG AUCTION

On the third Friday of every month or thereabouts, the gymnasium of the Crownpoint Elementary School is filled with Navajo artisans, browsers, and visitors at one of the best shopping – and cultural – opportunities on the res. This isn't oriented to tourists, but a major local social event that brings out friends and families for a fun night. Previewing runs 4–6 P.M., and students set up tables with snacks and drinks around 5 P.M. Artisans display jewelry, pottery, and other crafts in the halls, but inside the gym the focus is on rugs. You can pick up and examine any one that strikes your fancy and talk directly to its creator. Not only are prices lower here than just about anywhere else, but it is also a major source of income for the weavers, who get the money directly. Rugs sell for under $100 and up into the thousands. The auction starts at 7 P.M., and lasts until around midnight.

The school is in Crownpoint, 56 miles northeast of Gallup on the way to Chaco Canyon. Head north from Thoreau (I-40 exit 53) for 25 miles on Highway 371, turn left (west) at the Crownpoint sign, then take a right at the second four-way stop. The school is on the right – look for all the cars. Admission is free, and they don't take credit cards for purchases. For more information and to double-check the time and date, contact the **Crownpoint Rug Weavers Association** (505/786-7396, www.crownpointrugauction.com).

free). A sculpture of Manuelito, the famous 19th-century Navajo chief, stands in front of the large blue-and-gray building. On the second floor is the Storyteller Museum, with dioramas and displays on trading posts and native crafts, illustrated with great old black-and-white photos, and the Ceremonial Gallery, filled with modern Native American art. Films are shows in the Navajo Cinema, and you can grab a bite at the El Navajo Cafe (Mon.–Fri.), serving an inexpensive breakfast and lunch, including organic espresso drinks, on a wood table and chairs carved by the owner (they're also for sale). The gift shop, run by the Southwest Indian Foundation, stocks a good variety of crafts.

The Gallup Historical Society runs the **Rex Museum** (300 W. Hwy. 66, 505/863-1363, 8 A.M.–3:30 P.M. Mon.–Fri., $2 pp). in what was once the Rex Hotel (circa 1900). Vestiges of Gallup's mining heyday are on display inside nowadays.

The local Chamber of Commerce has brochures detailing a **walking tour** of historical Gallup. Some two dozen buildings downtown date to the early 20th century, including the 1925 **Grand Hotel** (306 W. Coal Ave); the "Pueblo Deco"–style **Chief Theater,** now the City Electric Shoe Shop (228 W. Coal Ave.); **Kitchen's Opera House** (218 W. Hwy. 66), built around 1890; and the ornate **El Morro Theater** (207 W. Coal Ave.), built in 1928 in the Spanish colonial revival style.

Events

All of Gallup's annual events are held at Red Rock State Park. The **Lion's Club Rodeo,** one of the state's best, arrives in June, but the biggest event of the year comes in August: the **Gallup Inter-Tribal Indian Ceremonial** (505/863-3896 or 800/233-4528). This event, called "The Greatest American Show" by none other than Will Rogers, has been held since 1922 and is one of the biggest of its kind. Members of more than 30 tribes come from as far away as Canada for four days of rodeos, dances, parades, and art displays. It's a good idea to get tickets ahead of time for this one:

Dances are $12–25, rodeos are $10, and to get on the grounds only will run you $3. The same goes for hotel reservations, which are booked solid months in advance.

Close to 200 hot-air balloons float skyward during the **Red Rock Balloon Rally** the first weekend in December. Free **Indian dances** are held for the public nightly from May–August at the cultural center.

Shopping

The real reason to spend time in Gallup is to browse the wares in the city's seemingly endless array of trading posts, art galleries, pawnshops, and gift stores. This is one of the Four Corners' top shopping destinations, and a stroll down Old Route 66 near the Santa Fe Train Depot is enough to burn a hole in the wallet of any devotee of southwestern arts and crafts. Of them all, **Richardson's Trading Company** (222 W. Hwy. 66, 505/722-4762, www.richardsontrading.com) is the most steeped in history—and around here, that's saying a lot. Opened in 1913, it stocks an

Gallup sidewalks evoke a bygone era.

overwhelming selection of crafts and goods from the wooden floor to the roof. At last count there were 2,000 rugs in the rug room, which is just behind the stuffed white buffalo (this one was bleached).

Perry Null Trading Co. (1710 S. 2nd St., 505/722-3806, www.pntrader.com) was started in 1939 as Tobe Turpen's Trading Post. They have tons of jewelry in the pawn vault, along with hundreds of pawned saddles. The Tanner family traces its trading history back to the arrival of Seth Tanner in the company of Brigham Young in the 19th century. Today, his fourth-generation descendants run some of Gallup's better stores: The **Ellis Tanner Trading Co.** (1980 Hwy. 602, 505/863-4434, www.etanner.com) stocks (among many other things) lots of pawned goods and paintings; and the **Shush Yaz Trading Co.** (1304 W. Lincoln, 505/722-0130, www.shushyaz.com) is named after Seth's son Don, nicknamed "Little Bear" by the Navajo. **Yazzie's Indian Art** (235 West Coal Ave., 505/726-8272) has a selection of outstanding jewelry.

Recreation

Gallup has started marketing itself as an outdoor destination as well as a cultural one, and with good reason. There are many hiking and biking trails, and even some good rock climbing, in the immediate vicinity. Two good trails start at **Red Rock State Park** (505/722-3829), 640 acres of beautiful scarlet canyons about six miles east of town via Route 66. (Head north on Highway 566, take another left after half a mile and follow the signs.) The **Pyramid Rock Trail** is a three-mile round-trip loop that takes you up to 7,500 feet, and the **Church Rock Trail** (two miles round-trip) offers views over sandstone towers. The park also has a 103-site campground ($12–18), a historical museum, and the 1888 Outlaw Trading Post.

The **Mentmore rock climbing area** features more than 80 bolted and top-climbs up to 45 feet high and 5.13 in difficulty. Find Mentmore Road by going half a mile west on Route 66 from I-40 exit 16, then turning north onto County Road 1, which becomes Mentmore

when it turns sharply left (west). Follow this another 1.5 miles up and over a hill, and continue straight through an open gate where the road veers right.

Behind the Gallup Community Service Center at 410 Bataan Veterans Street is the trailhead of the **Northside bike trail,** an 18-mile technical single-track ride through the piñon-and-juniper desert. Another good trail network open to bikers and hikers is the High Desert Trail System, accessed from the east at the Gamerco trailhead; head north three miles on Highway 491, turn left onto Chino Road, and turn left again after about 300 yards at the first road. **High Mesa Bikes** (123 W. Coal Ave., 505/863-3825) has maps and info.

Accommodations

Gallup has no shortage of hotel rooms, although some of the cheaper ones along Route 66, advertising rates as low as $15 per night, are better off avoided. There is one place in town you should stay if at all possible, or at least peek inside: the **El Rancho Hotel** (1000 E. Hwy. 66, 505/863-9311 or 800/543-6351, www.elranchohotel.com). It was opened in 1937 by D. W. Griffith's brother, and became a second home to movie stars filming nearby during the 1940s, '50s, and '60s. Ronald Reagan, Spencer Tracy, Kirk Douglas, and Katherine Hepburn all stayed here, and their signed photos grace the hallways today. It's a proud shrine to Hollywood's golden age of Westerns, with a flamboyant balconied lobby full of Native American art, big fireplaces, animal heads, and dark-wood furniture. Armand Ortega's Indian Store sells quality crafts, and live music floats from the 49er Lounge. Plates named after Carmen Miranda and Anthony Quinn are served at the restaurant, open daily for all meals. Rooms are $76–117, but rooms at the attached motel start at only $35.

For about $50, you can find a dependably clean and secure place at the **Economy Inn** (1709 W. Hwy. 66, 505/863-9301) and the **Red Roof Inn** (3304 W. Hwy. 66, 505/772-7765). In the $50–100 price range you'll also find a **Best Western Inn & Suites** (3009 W. Hwy.

66, 505/722-2221) and a **Days Inn** (3201 W. Hwy. 66, 505/863-6889). For camping choose Red Rock State Park, the **USA RV Park** (2925 W. Hwy. 66, 505/863-5021, www.usarvpark .com, $27–29), or the **KOA** (3900 E. Hwy. 66, 505/722-2333, $35–40).

Food

The parking lot is always packed at lunch at **Don Diego's Restaurant and Lounge** (801 W. Hwy. 66, 505/722-5517, all meals Mon.– Sat), which is a good sign that the Baca family is still cooking up the same great Mexican food they have been for decades. Dishes are $4–6 for breakfast, $6–8 for lunch, and $8–12 for dinner, including baby back ribs and carne adovada. There's a lounge with the "best margaritas in town," too. **Earl's Family Restaurant** (1400 E. Hwy. 66, 505/863-4201, all meals daily) is another local landmark, open since 1947. They serve inexpensive Mexican and American family fare.

For fine dining, the only game in town is **Chelles** (2201 W. Hwy. 66, 505/722-7698, dinner Mon.–Sat.). This place specializes in seafood, but they will also accommodate fans of Mexican cooking—a given this close to the border. They boast an extensive wine list and enticing desserts made in-house. **The Coffee House** (203 W. Coal Ave., 505/726-0291), next to the El Morro Theater, is open from 7 or 8 A.M. to 10 or 11 P.M. (10 A.M.–4 P.M. Sun.). Live music, poetry readings, and local art on the walls make it a cozy neighborhood spot, serving snacks and the usual caffeinated beverages. Western BBQ and Navajo tacos have been on the menu of **The Ranch Kitchen** (3001 W. Hwy. 66, 505/722-5696, all meals daily), for four decades, and **PeeWee's Kitchen** (1644 S. 2nd St., 505/863-9039, breakfast and lunch Mon.–Sat.) serves "family fare, cooked with care"—particularly the breakfasts.

Information and Transportation

For more information on Gallup and the surrounding area, contact the **Gallup-McKinley County Chamber of Commerce** (103 W. Hwy. 66, 505/722-2228, www.thegallupchamber .com). Gallup's **Greyhound** station is at 255 East Highway 66 (505/863-3761) and **Amtrak** is located at 201 East Highway 66 (505/863-3244).

WINDOW ROCK, ARIZONA

The administrative center of the Navajo Nation straddles the New Mexico/Arizona border 24 miles west of Gallup on Highway 264/3. It owes its importance to John Collier, commissioner of Indian Affairs in the 1930s, who brought the reservation's various offices together here as the Navajo Central Agency. He is remembered for his sympathetic ear in matters such as the tribe's education and health care, including the replacing of boarding schools with day schools for children.

Sights

The **Navajo Museum, Library, and Visitor Center** (928/871-7941, 8 A.M.–5 P.M. Mon.– Fri., to 8 P.M. Wed., 9 A.M.–5 P.M. Sat., free) is in the Navajo Arts and Crafts Enterprises building near the intersection of Highways 264/3 and 12. This large building houses a museum with sparse but well-done displays on tribal history, geology, and archaeology. Sharing the same parking lot are the **Navajo Parks & Recreation Department** (928/871-6647, www.navajonationparks.org, 8 A.M.–5 P.M.), where you can pick up permits for camping on the reservation, and the small **Navajo Zoological & Botanical Park** (928/871-6574, 10 A.M.–5 P.M. Mon.–Sat., free), which houses animals injured or otherwise unfit for the wild. The collection ranges from ducks and sheep to a cougar, black bears, bobcats, and one endlessly pacing wolf. (Pets are not allowed "for many reasons.")

The headquarters of the Navajo Tribal Government sit in front of **Window Rock Tribal Park** (928/871-6647, 8 A.M.–5 P.M. daily, free), centered around Tségháhoodzání, the "perforated pock," a natural window which figures in the Water Way ceremony. The park includes a sanctuary for healing and reflection with a sandstone fountain. The tribe's executive offices, council chamber, and police headquarters (for readers of Tony Hillerman's novels) are all here. To find it, take a right half a mile north of the intersection of Highways 264/3 and 12.

Shopping

A big selection including concha belts, books, jewelry, and craft supplies awaits at the **Navajo Arts & Crafts Enterprises** outlet (866/871-4095 or 928/871-4090, 9 A.M.–5 P.M. Mon.–Fri) near the Navajo Nation Inn. **Griswold's Inc** (1591A Hwy. 264, 928/371-5393) is between the KFC and the Napa Auto Parts store a few hundred yards east of Arizona/New Mexico line. Although it's only been in business since 1988, the front room is laid out in the classic bullpen design, and is full of locals cashing paychecks on Friday afternoons. They have a little of everything in stock, from cradle boards to saddles and pottery, as well as a few hundred rugs in the rug room.

Accommodations and Food

Most tourist activity in Window Rock centers around the **Quality Inn** (48 W. Hwy. 264, 928/871-4108 or 800/662-6189, www.explorenavajo.com, $70–80), a modest place with 56 rooms near the main intersection. The hotel's **Dine Restaurant** (all meals daily) is also the local favorite, serving good food (plates $6 and up) including a breakfast buffet, burgers, Navajo tacos (of course) and a good spicy roasted corn–chili soup. Other than that, your only choices are the Days Inn in St. Michaels and the bevy of fast-food outlets in Window Rock.

Information

The main office of the **Navajo Tourism Department** (928/810-8501, www.discover navajo.com) is in the governmental complex at Window Rock, although it's not a visitors center setup.

NORTH OF GALLUP
Highway 491

The northeastern corner of the Navajo Reservation is a stark lesson in geology. Heading north from Gallup, Highway 491 parallels the Chuska Mountains on the Arizona border, rising darkly to almost 10,000 feet. About 40 miles north of Gallup, Highway 134 heads west from Sheep Springs. On its way to Window Rock it crosses Washington Pass, named (to the chagrin of locals) after a U.S. Army soldier. Ten miles farther north on Highway 491 is a side road at Newcomb that quickly turns to dirt and leads 6.5 miles to the **Two Gray Hills Trading Post** (505/789-3270, www.twogreyhills.com, 8 A.M.–6 P.M. Mon.–Sat.). Les Wilson runs this timeless place, which was built in 1897 and gave its name to the distinctive white, black, and gray geometric rug pattern. Ask to see the small rug room in back, where he stocks a good selection made by local weavers. (If it looks closed, drive around back and honk your horn.)

The highway continues through a bizarre landscape of mesa, monoclines, and volcanic detritus. **Bennett Peak** and **Ford Butte,** on opposite sides of the highway near milepost 64, are both volcanic necks, left behind when softer outer layers eroded away, leaving the harder solid core behind. Dikes of hardened lava radiate from the necks like crazed bicycle spokes across the flat terrain.

To the north are **Rol-Hay Rock** to the west, sharp little **Barber Peak** and the **Hogback** monocline to the east, and then the main attraction, Shiprock.

Shiprock

There's not much to the town at the crossroads of Highways 64 and 491 of interest to tourists, aside from an impressive rock tower, a handful of fast-food restaurants, and a few good places to shop. The Foutz family, one of the oldest trading families on the reservation, runs the **Foutz Trading Co.** (505/368-5790 or 800/383-0615, www.foutzrug.com) with a good selection of Navajo folk art, knives with embroidered sheaths, and Navajo kachinas. The store is also full of craft supplies, including a colorful wall of yarn, and has separate rooms for rugs and sandpaintings. (There's

THE OWL, THE SNAKE, AND THE PILE OF WOOL

Monument Valley is just the beginning of the fascinating geology near Kayenta. Just north of Kayenta on Highway 163, **Agathla Peak** (6,096 feet) is a jagged volcanic neck with the same blackened, ominous look as Shiprock. This is believed to be the center of the Navajo world, set in place by the Holy People to prop up the sky. In Navajo, 'aghaa'lá means "much wool," and preserves the legend of a huge snake that made its home at the base of the rock. His wife, an owl, lived nearby – look for distinctive **Owl Rock** (6,547 feet) across the road, formed of Wingate Sandstone. The snake grew fat on the plentiful local antelope, and tossed so much leftover hair outside his home that the name stuck. Kit Carson later renamed the peak El Capitan, and the classic Western *Stagecoach* was filmed here in 1938.

Half Dome, which stands closer to Kayenta near **Church Rock** (5,580 feet), looms west of the town on Highway 160. Heading south along Highway 160 toward Tuba City, you'll pass along the south side of the **Organ Rock Monocline,** also called Skeleton Mesa. Huge sandstone teeth point northwest in the remains of this geologic uplift, raised 75-80 million years ago. **Marsh Pass** (6,750 feet) brings you to **Tsegi Canyon,** home to the Anasazi Inn. This beautiful canyon, coming in from the north, was carved by Laguna Creek and is relatively lush, with many Anasazi sites and fields of Navajo corn in summer. Highway 160 continues southwest through **Long House Canyon** to the turnoff for Navajo National Monument. An electric coal train passes over the road here, leading south to **Black Mesa** and the Peabody coal mines.

another Foutz Trading Co. on Highway 64 toward Farmington, across from a huge pile of scrap metal, but that one stocks mostly pawned goods.)

The town of Shiprock is also the home of the **Northern Navajo Fair** in early October, which brings a rodeo, powwow, traditional song and dance, a parade, and arts and crafts to the town fairgrounds. This colorful event has been going for almost a century, making it one of the oldest on the reservation.

The perfect impression of the inside of a volcano, **Shiprock** itself towers 1,700 feet above the desert, with a shape that explains why

the Navajo call it Tsé Bit' A'', the "rock with wings." The name, however, actually comes from a legend that tells how the Navajos' ancestors, praying for deliverance from their enemies far to the north, felt the ground rise up beneath their feet and carry them here. Other stories tell how the Hero Twins, Monster Slayer and Child Born For Water, scaled Shiprock to kill a nest full of monstrous birds that were preying on their people. Shiprock was first climbed by Anglos in 1939, but is now off-limits as a sacred site. (The English name comes from early Anglo settlers who were reminded of the sails of a 19th-century clipper ship.)

MOON NAVAJO & HOPI COUNTRY
Avalon Travel
a member of the Perseus Books Group
1700 Fourth Street
Berkeley, CA 94710, USA
www.moon.com

Editor: Shaharazade Husain
Series Manager: Kathryn Ettinger
Copy Editor: Emily Lunceford
Graphics Coordinator: Kathryn Osgood
Production Coordinator: Elizabeth Jang
Cover Designer: Kathryn Osgood
Map Editor: Kevin Anglin
Cartographers: Chris Markiewicz, Jon Niemczyk,
    Kat Bennett

ISBN: 978-1-59880-270-2

ABOUT THE AUTHOR

Julian Smith

"A life has to move or it stagnates."
Beryl Markham

Julian Smith has been writing since he learned to read, and traveling since his first family trip to Cape Cod as a toddler. A pre-college summer in Brazil sparked a love affair with Latin America, fueled by a stint studying the cloud forests of Costa Rica. Days after wrangling a degree in biology from the University of Virginia, he found himself hopelessly entangled in a self-publishing venture that resulted nine months later in the one-pound, eight-ounce *On Your Own in El Salvador*, the first in-depth guide to the country.

He has contributed to the *Smithsonian, Wired, Outside, National Geographic Traveler, National Geographic Adventure*, the *Washington Post*, the *Los Angeles Times, USA Today* and *U.S. News & World Report*. His first edition of Moon Four Corners won the country's top travel writing award from the Society of American Travel Writers. He also managed to earn a master's degree in wildlife ecology along the way, studying grizzly bear tourism on the coast of British Columbia.

As far as normal jobs go, Julian has done pretty well. He's launched and edited an international peer-reviewed scientific journal, guided tourists through the Central American rainforest, and tried (in vain) to protect the vegetable garden of one of the richest men in the world from marauding rodents. Along the way he's found himself freezing atop Kilimanjaro, meditating in a Japanese Zen temple, and fleeing from Ugandan pygmies, through absolutely no fault of his own. He lives in Portland, Oregon.

For more travel writing and photography, stop by his website (www.juliansmith.com) and his blog (juliansmith.typepad.com).